TURNING PRACTICAL
COMMUNICATION INTO
BUSINESS POWER

TURNING PRACTICAL COMMUNICATION INTO BUSINESS POWER

Bernard Katz

MERCURY

First published in 1989
by the Mercury Books Division of
W.H. Allen & Co. Plc
Sekforde House, 175--179 St. John Street, London EC1V 4LL.

Set in Meridien by Phoenix Photosetting
Printed and bound in Great Britain by
Mackays of Chatham PLC, Chatham, Kent

Cartoons by Alex Garland

British Library Cataloguing in Publication Data
Katz, Bernard, *1927–*
  Turning practical communication into business power.
  1. Business firms. Management. communication
  I. Title
  658.4'5

ISBN 1–85251–076–5

CONTENTS

Contents

TURNING PRACTICAL COMMUNICATION INTO BUSINESS POWER

INTRODUCTION

Understanding the meaning of communication is easy. We communicate every day, all the time. It is the same in business. Mostly, communication is taken for granted.

This book considers, in turn, the major ingredients of business communication. What are they? How are they best used? What practical help is available, in understandable terms, to make sure that communication is effective and clear.

The corporate body communicates although it is not a single person speaking. The environment in which a company operates has something to say too. Both can be influenced, so that the message that is given is louder and stronger. Added to this there are personal communication skills which, for most people, benefit from reinforcement. These pages are designed to make the reader even better when talking to or addressing others, conducting meetings or writing reports. And there are also words about audio-visual aids.

The book uses examples, checklists and rules to follow, and tells what should be avoided. This helps the reader to practise practical ways of enhancing personal skill. In chapter two a model training programme is set out. It is for the manager with little training practice wanting to train others to communicate more clearly.

At the beginning of each chapter there are a number of test questions. The reader is invited to use these questions as signposts, to identify topic areas of particular interest. The answers are then worked through in the body of the chapter. At the end of each chapter questions and answers are given together as a summary. Sometimes the reader's answer is going to differ from that given in the book. This does not mean that one is right and the other is wrong. The answers to some questions are a function of individual experience.

Hopefully, by the end of these pages there is a new high peak of communication excellence. In business, communication is all. It is the direct pathway to influencing others – and that is certainly power.

Bernard Katz
London
March 1989

1

THE PHYSICAL COMPANY ENVIRONMENT

QUESTIONS

What is communication in business?

What communication messages are given by the company environment?

What environment communication statements provide an immediate boost to company PR?

To what extent does physical environment administration contribute to company marketing activities?

A WORKING DEFINITION

Question: What is communication in business?

In simple terms, communication is an exchange of understanding. A sender gives a message to a receiver. Example: a railway guard waves a green flag. The signal means that it is safe to proceed.

Communication is also more complex. Birds are singing; there are buds on the trees. Young people skip in the street instead of walking. This is a message that it is springtime.

[3]

Communication in business is an exchange of ideas, messages and concepts, relating to the achievement of set commercial objectives. Ideally, messages communicated reach the receiver in the same format and with the same intensity as when they are sent. But this does not always happen. There are barriers to communication (see Fig. 1.1). The major barriers are:

(1) **the medium.** Is the message printed, announced or woven into fabric? Is it engraved or painted? Sometimes a message is an integral part of equipment or a process. How effectively a message is sent or a concept is transmitted is a function of the medium selected.

(2) **psychological factors.** The sender may have a different lifestyle or background to that of the receiver. Some customers will only make retail purchases on the basis of extended credit, using a card. 'Price' messages mean different things to the cash buyer and to the credit buyer.

(3) **educational factors.** Language that is too complex may not be understood. As a general rule, in business language, words should be simple, sentences short.

(4) **cultural factors.** Messages are distorted from their original intent because of the influence of culture filtering the perceived image. Example: in France the colour yellow has the significance of infidelity. This makes it an inappropriate colour for the packaging of some products.

(5) **listening skills.** Attention must not be distracted from the message that is being communicated. Lack of concentration filters or distorts messages. Poor listening is as dramatic in its consequences as blurred vision.

EXTERNAL COMMUNICATION SIGNALS

Question: What communication messages are given by the company environment?

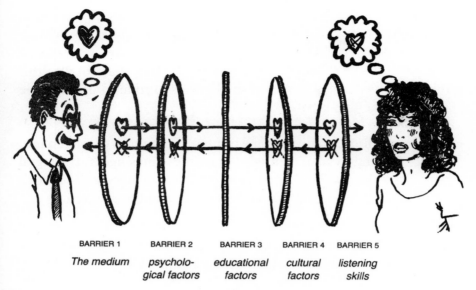

BARRIER 1	BARRIER 2	BARRIER 3	BARRIER 4	BARRIER 5
The medium	*psycholo-gical factors*	*educational factors*	*cultural factors*	*listening skills*

FIG. 1.1   *Barriers to Communication*

A few company environmental statements are written. For example, the company signboard says who the company is. Direction indicators tell visitors where to go. Most environmental communication statements are non-verbal. They fall into three major categories:

(1) Location (2) environment scheduling (3) environment administration.

(1) Location

With some prestigious sites, for example in London next to the Bank of England, or in the heart of Mayfair, the message to all is loud and clear. 'We are an important company with high status because we occupy property of very high rental value.' Other specific locations are adopted by industries and professions. Consulting engineers, medical consultants, fishmongers, diamond merchants all crowd within identifiable districts or streets. There is an implicit message in these circumstances too. 'We are an important company because we are based where all the others in our trade or profession are based.'

When a location carries an image tag recognisable by all, the communication aspects of that location are valuable. For other geographical areas, factors different to communication have formed the basis for selection. Typical other factors are costs, or proximity to transport services or to local staff.

(2) Environment Scheduling

Environment scheduling is how the workplace of a company is set out in the context of the geographical surroundings. Ideally factories and offices are part of an idyllic sculpted landscape. There is water and there are trees and grass. Each blends harmoniously with office and factory walls.

From such pleasing visual images positive messages are given to visitors and company personnel alike. 'This company is successful!' 'Working conditions are superb!' 'What a bonus it must be to work in such conditions!'

But some organisations work from the same shop floor, the same reception and office areas and the same car park spaces that have served them for the last ten or twenty years. The communication messages from such environments are often counter-productive to an image of progress.

When concern for the communication aspects of environment scheduling has low priority, it is time to institute change. The following audit checklist can be used to evaluate the level of concern:

Audit Checklist of Environment Scheduling

Place a tick in appropriate square   YES   NO

- Are the company premises visually pleasing?   ☐   ☐

[6]

	YES	NO
• Are walkway surfaces made up, and protected from the weather?	☐	☐
• Is the company entrance inviting?	☐	☐
• Is access for people, goods and vehicles well planned?	☐	☐
• Are there adequate car parking facilities?	☐	☐
• Is the decorative condition of company premises, inside and out, of an acceptably high standard?	☐	☐
• Are booking/information counters well situated?	☐	☐
• Is there unused land with potential for landscaping?	☐	☐
• Have lifts been installed to provide access to upper floors?	☐	☐
• Have the social and visual aspects of equipment siting been considered?	☐	☐
• Has cosmetic upgrading been considered lately?	☐	☐

If the answer is YES, O.K. If NO do something about it!

(3) Environment Administration

Environment administration is the way the environment is managed. It is the day to day range of communication messages that are given to all who work in and visit the company premises. The messages are generated by routine activities, efficiently carried out:

- The reception area is kept tidy.

- No deliveries are stacked, or paperwork stored in the waiting area.

- Ashtrays are kept clean.

- Daily papers and journals are up to date issues.

- Toilets are kept clean and in good repair.

- Facilities are available to deposit visitors' coats and umbrellas.

- A telephone is available for the use of visitors.

- There is a telephone 'hot line' to help customers in product usage.

- Company cars are maintained in immaculate condition.

- Directions are prominently signposted.

- Staff uniforms and personal dress are neat and tidy.

- Any public address system used is clearly audible.

- Company literature is prominently available to visitors.

ADDED VALUE COMMUNICATION

Question: What environment communication statements provide an immediate boost to company PR?

When a company is good, it should say so. And it should care. In the history of a company there are many different records of company achievements. They exist for the company. They exist for personnel. But the triumphs are transient. It requires application to identify such trophies. Inertia quickly relegates records of success to cupboards and files, to await attention. Mostly such attention takes second place to the day to day demands. Examples that can be used to promote the company *now* are:

- Press cuttings and photographs. They should be professionally framed and displayed prominently.

- Membership and award certificates of industry and professional bodies. They must be in view on the walls. They increase credibility.

- Samples of products and product literature must be shown. These are why the company is successful.

- Visitors should be offered refreshment – coffee or tea or a cold drink. The cost is negligible compared to the value of the image created.

A MARKETING EDGE

Question: To what extent does physical environment administration contribute to company marketing activities?

Marketing means putting the customer first. It is finding out what the customer really wants and then selling the product or service that satisfies those needs.

The pathway to successful marketing is through control and deployment of marketing variables. The most important variables are known in marketing terms as the marketing mix. They are the **four Ps and an S** – PRODUCT, PRICE, PLACE, PROMOTION and SERVICE. They are illustrated in Fig. 1.2. The task of marketing is to concentrate on these variables and get them right – both in terms of meeting objectives, and staying within apportioned budgets.

Product. The format of the product or core service is developed to match what the customer wants, in every aspect. It is the right size, shape, weight, quality, colour, and degree of sophistication. These details are identified by research.

Price. Price is a function of many factors. It is variable and fixed costs plus a percentage profit. It is a price set to undercut competitors, or discourage new suppliers. It is quoted at a level to accommodate intensive promotion. Management decides what the price is to be.

Place. Place is where the goods or service are offered to customers and potential customers. Companies make use of different channels of distribution to reach the end users. For example, similar goods may be sold through retail outlets, by mail order, from a travelling van at the kerbside, or by a door to door salesman.

Promotion. Customer awareness is achieved through promotion. Advertising, publicity and premium gifts are all examples of promotion. Within the marketing budget appropriations, management decides what promotional activities are going to enhance sales performance.

Service. Peripheral service, provided at first contact to members of the public and customers alike, is an important influencing factor in the customer purchase decision. Peripheral service, when planned and provided efficiently, sets the scene. It allays apprehension. This allows the customer to be moved along the purchase decision making process, from 'disinterest' to a point nearer to the 'buy' decision.

Physical environment administration contributes to marketing through the service aspect of the marketing mix. Examples are:

- **Car parking arrangements.** Adequate space and clear signposting are essential ingredients. Visitors want to know where to go, and how to reach the 'Reception' point.

- **Livery.** Co-ordinated style and colour of premises, company vehicles and staff uniforms are remembered, albeit nowadays they are relatively rare. Livery must be neat and tidy at all times, because it has an impact on all who see it.

- **Public address system.** Care must be taken that the positive benefits of the public address system are not neutralised by poor tone or ambiguous messages. The advantages of an efficient system are the provision of up to date and routine information, and opportunities to sell.

- **Suggestion box.** A suggestion box is an opportunity to contact and influence management. It is important. It means that the company cares about the opinions of both staff and customer.

- **Visitor toilet and wash room facilities.** Well kept facilities earn immediate good public relations points for the company from visitors.

- **Information desk.** Depending on the industry, there is a need to accommodate customers with a complaint, or those wishing to exchange or return purchases. A counter marked **'Complaints'** is unlikely to be provided, but an easily accessible **'Information'** counter is sure to neutralise the stress of customers feeling aggrieved.

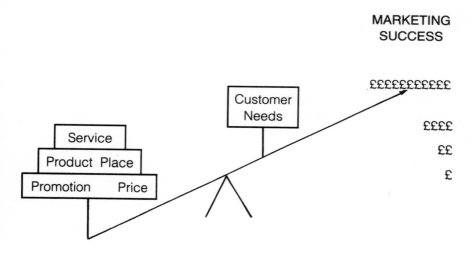

FIG. 1.2 *Four Ps and an S.* *The Marketing Mix Variables for Marketing Success*

SUMMARY

Question: What is communication in business?

Answer: Communication in business is an exchange of ideas, messages and concepts, relating to the achievement of set commercial objectives.

Question: What communication messages are given by the company environment?

Answer: Environmental communication statements fall into three main categories – (1) location (2) environment scheduling and (3) environment administration. Such statements are mostly non-verbal.

Question: What environment communication statements provide an immediate boost to company PR?

Answer: Environment statements reflecting the achievements, successes and activities of a company contribute to good PR and should be seen by all.

Question: To what extent does physical environment administration contribute to company marketing activities?

Answer: Physical environment administration is the Service variable in the marketing mix of 4 Ps and an S. Marketing activities include car parking arrangements, livery, public address system, suggestion box, visitor toilet facilities and an information desk.

2

WHAT IS GOING ON IN
THE COMPANY?

QUESTIONS

In what ways do communication messages flow within a business?

What are the problems created by poor communication?

What are the tools for monitoring levels of communication effectiveness?

What kind of training heightens staff awareness of the importance of communication?

COMMUNICATION FLOW

Question: In what ways do communication messages flow within a business?

Communication is the life blood of a company. It flows downwards through the company as top management tells line management and personnel what to do. Communication flows upwards. Management learns how customers in the marketplace react; how the workforce thinks. Good vertical communication flow is essential to policy decision making. Communication flows laterally as well at different levels within the company. In addition, there is the grapevine, nourished by rumours, linking all levels of a company.

Within each flow direction there are major communication channels:

Downwards flow – management communicates downwards through

- company rules
- manuals
- the job specification

This communication is important but it is static. More dynamic communication, reflecting day to day change, is accomplished through

- presentations
- advisory meetings
- the company noticeboard
- letters
- house magazine
- newsletter
- appraisal interviews

Upwards flow – one of the most important channels in upward communication flow is reporting. Reports are made formally in writing and are also presented verbally. Communication upwards is achieved as well through management/staff councils and by memoranda.

Lateral flow – sideways or lateral communication passes through social relationships built up from continuous workday contact.

Memoranda, face to face conversations, telephone conversations and meetings are the channels. Companies encouraging sporting or cultural activities outside of working hours and offering resources to promote such activities do much to help lateral communication flow. Network relationships grow too in large organisations. Individuals finding rapport with others in different work activities maintain such relationships. The network relationship is essentially two-way, with mutual pleasure arising from occasional contact.

PROBLEMS ARISING

Question: What are the problems created by poor communication?

Poor communication within a company as a whole is not always readily identifiable. Poor communication is often made up of a number of small single items:

- a memorandum is misdirected

- a letter is not posted

- customers have difficulty in making contact

- telephone messages are not passed on

- visitors cannot find their way around

- customers do not know the range of company activities other than for their own specific contact

In each individual case it is a single person that is involved or affected. The response of irritation or indifference is transient. Customers and potential customers may try to communicate again. Often they just go away. But there is no register telling management that this week the company lost £50,000 of potential business through poor communication.

Poor communication may be the cause of:

- high telephone bills

- high product return rate

- strikes

- low staff morale

- high industrial accident rate

- falling sales

- low market share

Evaluating communication effectiveness is as important as monitoring and analysing financial performance. It provides a pathway for management to increase motivation, to rectify or enhance management control, and to lay the bedrock for development and progress.

MEASURING COMMUNICATION LEVELS

Question: What are the tools for monitoring levels of communication effectiveness?

There are three major methods of carrying out an audit of communication effectiveness:

(1) Analysing communication structure through interview and by questionnaire

This approach varies as a function of the company or organisation and the communication problem identified. For every interview or questionnaire programme there must be precise objectives. The following checklist is provided as a starting point for an audit tailored to individual circumstance:

Checklist For Evaluating Communication Effectiveness

- What lines of communication permit optimum communication flow?

- What known communication constraints are a function of human error, incompetence or inadequacy?

- What known communication constraints relate to technological malfunction?

- What is the geographical basis for poor communication?

- What effect does work scheduling have on communication? (Manning of the telephone switchboard at lunchtime is a particularly sensitive area.)

- How much do staff wage and bonuses influence communication?

- What effect does staff turnover have on communication effectiveness?

- What is the nature and frequency of training that is likely to offer improved communication?

(2) Preparation of a sociogram (network map)

There are informal communication links that transcend traditional organisational pathways. Knowledge of a football pool win, of personal honour or mishap spread throughout an organisation very quickly indeed. The news travels along a network path different to that followed, for example, by an announcement of changes in company car parking arrangements. Communication in the latter circumstance is slow and prone to disruption.

A sociogram is a drawing of a communication network. It is illustrated in Fig. 2.1. Well defined roles are seen.

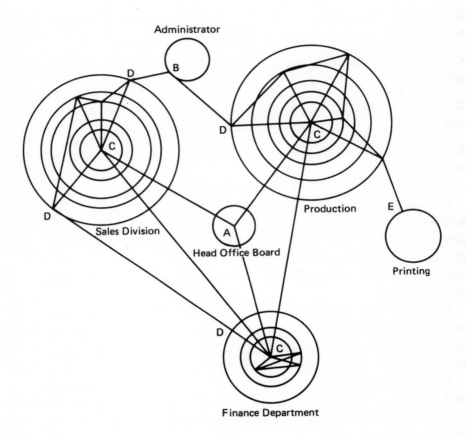

FIG. 2.1   *Sociogram Network*

A is a clique or group who communicate mostly amongst themselves

B links two or more cliques or groups without personally belonging to a clique

C is a communication leader with communication links to many others

D is a member of one communication clique linking it with another clique

E is isolated having minimal communication contact with the organisation

Structured information is gathered to plot a sociogram by observation and by question. Each of the persons involved is asked how frequently he or she has spoken contact with each of the other persons named. Responses are in the categories of 'zero', 'few' or 'many'. 'Few' or 'many' are quantified depending on the particular circumstances.

Decisions must be made, when designing the audit, as to whether contact means business related or non-business related conversations. All the responses obtained are then interpreted in diagrammatic form.

For management the sociogram resulting from a communication audit tells how communication flow deviates from traditional paths. It is then possible, where appropriate, to restructure communication channels within the company.

(3) Personal diary audit

In an ideal industrial and commercial environment, each division or department of a company knows what the other is doing. In many cases a lack of effective two-way communication significantly impedes progress. Example: the service department and sales department of a company supplying office equipment benefit from feedback on each other's performance. Sales can advise when particular equipment is likely to need specific reinforcement in terms of servicing or spare part inventory. The service department is well placed to observe opportunities arising for customer expansion. A lead to the sales office may then result in a contract for additional equipment.

So the diary audit is designed to identify communication information pertinent to a company and its activities. Fig. 2.2 illustrates a Communication Diary Audit page. Across the top of the diary page are heading entries of different communication media: telephone, memoranda, face to face meetings, letters, social meetings.

Subjects are invited or cajoled into keeping the diary for a short period. Every time communication contact occurs a tick is entered in the appropriate square. Subdivisions of 'self' and 'other' within each column identify the originator of the communication contact. Generally, enthusiasm flags when the diary is kept for longer than one week.

Analysis of the information provided by diary audits is helpful in two ways:

(1) There are pointers to blockages and gaps in communication flow. These can be rectified through structured meetings and training.

(2) Management becomes aware of fast communication pathways. These are valuable in motivating or stabilising staff.

IMPROVING STANDARDS

Question: What kind of training heightens staff awareness of the importance of communication?

Few people dispute that training is important. Some accept the principle but believe that for their busy office or department it is not really appropriate. Furthermore, training is a skill. Managers without experience in training are reluctant to expose a possible weakness.

[20]

Name................................ From................. To................

Day	PHONE Self	PHONE Other	MEMORANDUM Self	MEMORANDUM Other	FACE-TO-FACE Self	FACE-TO-FACE Other	LETTER Self	LETTER Other	SOCIAL MEETING Self	SOCIAL MEETING Other	TOTALS	VALUE TO COMPANY Zero	VALUE TO COMPANY Little	VALUE TO COMPANY Much
Monday														
Tuesday														
Wednesday														
Thursday														
Friday														
Saturday														
Sunday														

Each day enter a tick for each communication contact source. When value of communication activities is high, encircle the most important communication activities.

The evaluation of this diary, in conjunction with the diaries of others in the company, is undertaken with the objective of improving communication flow within the company. Your cooperation is appreciated.

FIG. 2.2 *Communication Diary Audit Sheet*

Most successful training occurs when participants in the training environment do something themselves. Learning by doing is far more successful than learning by watching or just listening. Fun training is a bonus. Participants enjoy the training game, losing awareness that they are in a structured learning environment.

The following session, built on a game, is designed to help participants identify the nature and constraints of communication and to reinforce their own skills.

Communication Training Session

Venue: Room with space to accommodate participants arranged in small syndicate groups of three or four persons.

Equipment: Flip chart paper and easel. Crayons. Overhead slide projector and screen. Tutor's table. Participant tables and chairs.

Pre-training Session Communication:

MEMORANDUM

To: John Smith

From: Self

Date: 15th June

....

Subject: COMMUNICATION TRAINING SESSION. Friday 23rd June

Conference Room 9.00–11.00 a.m.

A training session has been developed to improve communication effectiveness within the company. You are invited to attend.

Please arrange that all calls and messages for you are taken by others, so that the session is not interrupted.

Training Resources:

1. Overhead slide no. 1: 'Communication Fields of Buyer and Seller' Fig. 2.3.

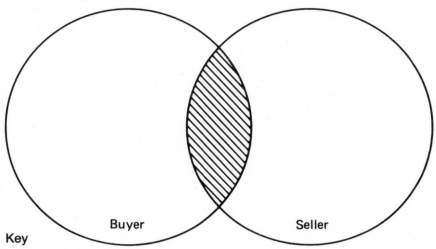

Key

Shaded portion represents area
of optimum communication

FIG. 2.3   *Slide no. 1: Communication Fields of Buyer and Seller*

2. Overhead slide no. 2: 'Barriers to Communication' Fig. 1.1 (p. 5).

3. Sheets of plain white A4 paper, pens, pencils, rubbers, red coloured pencils, handout folder.

4. Handout no. 1:

OBJECTIVES

By the end of this session participants have:

    (a) become familiar with the barriers to communication

    (b) identified personal strengths and weaknesses in communication

    (c) developed a checklist of behaviour designed to improve communication skills

5. Handout no. 2: Photocopy of overhead slide no. 1 (p. 23).

6. Handout no. 3: Photocopy of overhead slide no. 2 (p. 5).

7. Handout no. 4: Exercise: Barriers to Communication:

In class the barriers to good communication have been discussed. Your task, working in syndicate, is to prepare a checklist entitled: *How To Overcome Barriers To Communication*. Record your answers on a sheet of flip chart paper. Appoint a representative to present that checklist to the group.

Use the space below to record the checklist items of others that complement your own list.

HOW TO OVERCOME BARRIERS TO COMMUNICATION

....

....

....

....

....

....

....

....

....

....

....

....

---

8. Design for communication game: Fig. 2.4 (p. 26).

9. Handout no. 5: Communication Game:

After playing the game set by your tutor, in syndicate prepare a checklist entitled *How To Improve Personal Communication Skills*. Record your list on a sheet of flip chart paper. Appoint a representative to present your list to the group. Use the space below to copy those items from other lists that are complementary to your own.

HOW TO IMPROVE PERSONAL COMMUNICATION SKILLS

....
....
....
....
....
....
....
....

Tutor Notes
(1) Welcome class and introduce yourself.

(2) Tell class that a training course has to have a structure. So you have written the objectives to be achieved by the end of the session. Distribute handout no. 1.

Each person is to put a tick against the objective that is most important for them, and a cross against the objective that is least important. Never mind what the neighbour does: individual opinions are required.

Meantime, write 'Most important' and 'Least important' at the top of a flip chart.

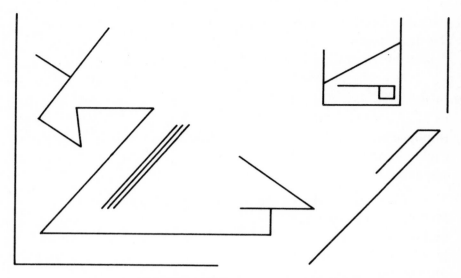

FIG. 2.4   *Random Design for Communication Game Exercise*
(Design can usefully be photocopied and enlarged to A4 size.)

(3) Go round the class and record the numbers representing the most important and least important choice of each participant. Comment briefly that communication effectiveness varies from person to person. Uniform opinion within the class is unlikely to occur. The exercise is simply to show how the group thinks.

(4) Illustrate overhead slide no. 1 (p. 23). Explain that in a sales situation the seller is in command of his or her own space. This is represented by the 'seller' circle. The space reflects product knowledge, the seller's professionalism, product application, product benefits – everything pertaining to the seller's world.

Similarly the circle marked 'buyer' represents the buyer's space. It reflects all that the buyer needs and wants. The two circles overlap. The greater the overlap, the better the understanding by the seller of what the buyer wants; and the more clearly the buyer sees how the seller's product can be a source of satisfaction.

Overlap in conceptual terms is a function of communication. So the more clearly one communicates in a sales situation the greater is the overlap achieved, and the more chance of securing a sale.

Distribute handout no. 2 for participants to keep.

(5) Illustrate overhead slide no. 2 (p. 5). Invite participants in turn to interpret the different barriers to communication. After each response bring in the rest of the class by asking 'Is that a complete explanation?' or 'How do you amplify that answer?' or 'What else can be said?'

(6) Tell the class that they are now going to carry out an exercise to find ways of overcoming such barriers. Distribute handouts 3 and 4 (p. 24). Divide group into syndicates. Say that there is 25 minutes to complete the exercise.

(7) After time is up assemble class. Invite each syndicate in turn to present their checklist. Ask one or two questions as each list is presented. Encourage and thank each presenter.

(8) Now the group is going to practise communicating. They are going to play a game in which some of the senses are restricted. At the end of the game the problems are discussed. A further checklist on communicating effectively is then to be developed, based on individual experience. Distribute handout no. 5 (p. 25).

Game: An artist, appointed within each syndicate, is to reproduce a design located at a distant point. The artist is not allowed to look at the original design. Information must be communicated by syndicate members. No pointing is allowed. Only the artist in each syndicate is allowed to draw. No note taking or sketching by others is permitted.

The design figure 2.4 is placed on the tutor's desk. Each syndicate artist is provided with A4 white paper, pencil, rubber, ruler and coloured pencil. When ready, one member from each syndicate proceeds to the tutor's desk to observe the design. He or she then returns to the syndicate base to instruct the artist. The next member of the syndicate goes to the design and the process is repeated.

Members may go backwards and forwards between the design and the artist as frequently as desired, but only one person from any syndicate is allowed at the design at any one time.

Players must keep their hands behind their backs. This prevents pointing and drawing in the air.

When the exercise is concluded and the design has been copied invite the artists to compare their work with the original. Assemble class. Ask each artist in turn what communication problems or difficulties have been experienced. Ask the others to describe the difficulties they experienced in communicating to the artists.

(9) Lead short discussion on solutions to communication problems raised so that in setting class task of preparing checklist *How To Improve Personal Communication Skills* all know what to do. Allow twenty minutes.

(10) Assemble class for presentation of each syndicate checklist.

(11) Conclude training session with summary of what has been covered. Ask each participant to write on a piece of paper three ways in which they are now going to improve their communication skills. As soon as ready, go round class to obtain individual communication improvement commitments.

SUMMARY

Question: In what ways do communication messages flow within a business?

Answer: Within a business, communication messages flow through channels in three directions – downwards from management at the top, upwards by written and verbal reporting, and laterally. In addition an informal grapevine interweaves all three channels.

Question: What are the problems created by poor communication?

Answer: Poor communication may be the cause of many industrial ills, including high telephone bills, high product return rate, strikes, low staff morale, high industrial accident rate, falling sales and a low market share.

Question: What are the tools for monitoring levels of communication effectiveness?

Answer: Three important tools for measuring levels of communication effectiveness are:
(1) analysis of the communication structure through interview and questionnaire
(2) Development of a sociogram
(3) Keeping a personal diary audit

Question: What kind of training heightens staff awareness of the importance of communication?

Answer: Effective training is interactive training where participants learn by individual action and involvement. The application to communication is through a game where constraints impose difficulties in the way of normal communication.

3

MAKING AN EXCELLENT PRESENTATION

QUESTIONS

What is the best way of preparing for a presentation?

What is a practical format for a presentation?

What helps to turn an ordinary presentation into an excellent presentation?

How are visual aids used to best effect?

What personal techniques are displayed by the accomplished speaker?

What is the best way of perfecting a presentation?

GETTING READY

Question: What is the best way of preparing for a presentation?

Making a personal presentation means standing up and speaking. In business the presentation takes a number of forms. It includes selling; it covers providing information. It is also in the literal sense giving a diploma or a cup to a recipient, and then following it with an appropriate speech. Other forms of presentation are proposing a toast, or making an after dinner speech.

In all cases the speech is prepared for a target audience. Who is the speech for? Is the audience made up of a board of directors? Are there managers, overseas guests, or the workforce? The audience has an influence on the language that is used. And it influences the delivery that is most effective in achieving a desired reaction or outcome.

There is a set of rules to structure preparation for making a presentation. In the above discussion the first rule has been described:

Rule No. 1. Identify the target audience for the presentation.

A presentation has a purpose. It may be to sell a particular product or concept, or to announce management changes. Perhaps it is to motivate; or warn against a course of action. There are many different reasons for making a presentation.

Identify the reason for the presentation. That is an early priority. The subject matter reflecting the reason is then developed in a format that the audience is going to understand. So in practical terms key points are first identified. It is best to write them down. What information about the speaker is appropriate? What facts have to be given to the audience? What opinions or suggestions should be made. What instructions are to be put forward in respect of action to be taken.

Rule No. 2. List the key points of the presentation.

At this stage, the experienced speaker, and those tentatively experimenting with the task, do different things. The experienced speaker needs little more than a list of key points on a card.

Those with less experience should write out the speech in full. This allows the opportunity for relaxed self criticism. It also gives the opportunity to ask a friend or member of the family for an opinion.

Rule No. 3. Write out the speech in full.

Making a speech, for those who do not make speeches, is a hurdle. Speechmaking is a skill that can be learned. For some it is shrouded in terror, and an erroneous belief that the task is insurmountable.

One option the less experienced speaker sees is to stand up and read the written out speech. It is not an option to be considered. Reading is not speechmaking. Sadly it happens all too frequently. For reasons of company politics or courtesy, the audience response to poor speechmaking is often enthusiastic. There is much clapping and approval. But it does not signify that the level of delivery is good.

The full written speech has to be condensed. With a highlight pen, the opening sentence of each paragraph, and the salient points within each paragraph are marked.

The speech is then read, and re-read, so that the overall structure, the order of paragraphs and the substance of each paragraph are memorised. Speechmaking at the beginning, and even when you are something of an expert, requires rehearsal and more rehearsal.

When there is familiarity, the condensed speech is written out again, only in its new form of paragraph headings and major points.

Some speakers choose to retain the full written speech as their form of notes, with the intention of using the bold highlighted phrases to help their memory. There are two arguments against this. (1) Large sheets of paper tend to rustle, which is distracting for the audience. (2) If the place is lost, it is difficult to find it whilst still speaking.

Ideally, the full speech, condensed down into headings and trigger phrases is written on postcard sized cards. These can be held in one hand, and do not intrude. A hole should be punched in the corner of the cards and a tag used to connect them together. If the cards are dropped, and the speaker picks them up out of sequence, he or she may have added an unwanted problem.

Rule No. 4. Condense speech to headings and triggerwords. Write them on a set of postcard sized cards.

THE BEST FORMAT

Question: What is a practical format for a presentation?

Every presentation, every speech, has to have a beginning, a middle and an end. The reason is so that the presentation is given to the audience in easily digestible sections.

Beginning

The first section prepares the audience. The audience is told what they are going to hear in a series of ordered steps:

(1) Welcome
The audience is greeted in a confident, authoritative manner. Smiling always helps. Any person who has introduced the speaker is thanked for what he or she has said.

(2) Self identification
The speaker tells the audience who he or she is – experience, why invited to talk – and the status and tasks of any colleagues helping in the presentation. Matching the speaker's experience to that of the audience is of far greater value than striving for factual exactitude. 'I am an expert in water sewage treatment. I am now going to talk to you about flower arrangements.' A moment's thought about what is appropriate is all that is needed.

(3) Purpose
The objectives of the presentation are given and the audience is told how the presentation will benefit them.

(4) Route map
The route map covers the main points to be dealt with in the presentation. In this way the audience is signposted from the very start and knows which topics are going to be covered and in what order.

(5) Procedure
The speaker tells the audience when they may ask questions, and
when interruptions and discussion are welcome. If there are handouts, or if literature has been distributed, the speaker gently but
firmly tells the audience when they may be read.

Middle

The middle section is the body of the speech. It is where arguments
are laid, and praises praised. The beginning and the end of a presentation are vehicles to carry and present this very important part. So
there must be order in the middle section.

(1) Set the scene. Describe the circumstances and details within
which the actions to be proposed are set.
   Example: The merger with ABCD Ltd has provided opportunities
for the development of the new XI model.

(2) Identify the main problem. What is the major topic that the
presentation is addressing?
   Problem: Which export market should the company tackle.

(3) Consider the important options.
Option 1. Japan. A large affluent market. Market entry sure to be
difficult with a lead time of five years before profitability can be
reached.
   Option 2. Eastern United States. Company already has a presence
in the market, but the hardening of currency exchange rates is a
serious obstacle.
   Option 3. 1992 Single European Market. Geographical proximity
is a persuasive consideration.

(4) Present the proposal.
Example: 'Gentlemen. My proposal is that resources are
immediately allocated for a market launch in France. We have
strong distribution channels there, and an excellent track record.

But I propose also that in parallel, in-depth market research for future market entry in Japan be commissioned.'

End

Evidence has been presented, arguments unfolded, options considered and a proposal made. What is more, the signposts signalled at the outset have been used to tell the audience where they are at each stage.

The close should be constructed so that the audience are in no doubt as to what they should do.

'So, Gentlemen, please consider the case I have put before you. The future of our company is in your hands. Please help progress in the most effective way by supporting the marketing launch into the Single European Market.'

Even if no direct action is desired, a first class presentation leaves the audience thinking and talking about what they have just heard.

SPECIAL INGREDIENTS

Question: What helps to turn an ordinary presentation into an excellent presentation?

In a good presentation, the speaker is in control of his or her audience at all times. In part, this is a function of confidence and experience. The novice speaker lacks confidence. But it is possible to act out the role of a confident speaker, by pausing, and maintaining continuous eye contact with the audience, even though the stomach is churning and the body trembling.

Very important ingredients of a good speech are a strong opening and a strong close. Laughter is an excellent pathway to the strong opening and close. This does not necessarily exclude all of us unblessed with instant penetrating wit. Aphorisms, quotations, and the witty sayings of others can be collected. Most reputable bookshops have a section with the published sayings of outstanding speakers. A small notebook is all that is necessary. Whenever something witty is heard at a presentation or dinner, it is recorded.

The following openings and closes have generated laughter:

'Ladies and Gentlemen. As Henry VIII said to his wives, I shan't keep you very long.'

'The brain is a marvellous piece of engineering. It serves the body perfectly, from the moment you are born, right up to the time you stand to make a speech.'

'. . . and this welcome success has been achieved in our company through the practice of Sunshine Management. You all know what that is! Sunshine Management. It is "Do it my way, Sunshine".'

'. . . and whilst looking for spiritual approval for our actions we should remember the famous words of Mae West who said "God is love! But get it in writing".'

Many speakers create stress for themselves when their proposed sequence of words is altered. In preparation, a particular route through the presentation has been selected. Speakers immediately worry when they realise that they have omitted a section, or spoken on topics in the wrong order. Speakers worry even though they have corrected and balanced their presentation with immaculate aplomb. The public is rarely aware that anything is wrong: they are not privy to the preparations (or agonies) of the speaker.

VISUAL AIDS

Question: How are visual aids used to best effect?

Visual aids reinforce a presentation. They should be planned for just that task, not to take over from the presenter. The good speaker

[37]

simplifies all complex material to make it easily understandable. Visual aids help that process by providing emphasis and reinforcement through sight, to go hand in hand with the spoken word.

In business the following visual aids are used to good effect:

Flip Charts

Flip charts are used to display headings or diagrams or charts. A single word or a phrase concentrates the attention of the audience. The speaker can write it at the same time as talking. But care is needed. The speaker must never stand with his or her back to the audience writing or reading. It is a common pitfall.

Flip chart sheets may also be prepared in advance, and disclosed when needed. The audience should not be allowed to see the prepared sheet before the relevant point in the presentation is reached. Otherwise the impact is diminished. It is helpful to fold over the bottom left hand corner of the prepared sheet. This avoids fumbling when trying to locate the exact sheet.

Writing should always be in thick bold crayon. Different colours should be used. Headings are best underlined to make them stand out.

It is possible to write relevant data needed by the speaker, or short prompts, in pencil on the flip chart sheet. This writing is not seen by anyone more than two or three feet away. So it allows the person presenting to dispense with notes. But particular care has to be taken that the speaker does not stand peering at the flip chart to find the notes, or reading facing away from the audience.

Overhead Slide Projectors

A commonly used slide is 25 cm × 25 cm. It is projected on a screen. A slide that has been professionally prepared, using more than one colour, has dramatic effect in a presentation. The attention of the audience is held the moment it is shown. The speaker then takes over and leads. Careful planning of a series of slides allows the presenter to dispense with notes entirely. Trigger words, headings or pictures on each slide prompt the speaker with the material to be presented.

The slides can be mounted in a cardboard frame. So additional prompt words for the presenter can be written on the frame. Overhead slides are easy to use. Portable projectors are available. Many projectors have the facility of a continuous roll of acrylic film. Writing or drawing on the film is displayed at the same time on the screen. This gives the presenter the advantage of facing the audience whilst drawing.

35 mm Projector Slides

Professional photographic slides have their place in many presentations. Examples are with cultural, scientific, academic and geographical subjects. Sophisticated equipment can take over from the presenter with a linked pre-recorded commentary, as also with complex visual fade-out sequencing.

One important rule applies to the presenter whether the 35 mm projector equipment is of the highest sophistication or inherited from the time of the Second World War. It is *rehearse!* Equipment malfunctions. Equipment fails to work through unfamiliarity with operating procedures. Furthermore, slides have a predilection for being inserted upside down in reverse order.

Computer Graphics

The equipment needed is a micro computer, Barco type projector, screen, and appropriate software. Computer graphics are dramatic when seen on a video monitor. This effect is magnified considerably when the image becomes screen size.

The graphics are planned as an integral part of a presentation. There is application, for example, in drawing conclusions from activities or projected investigations. Options and results are seen in colour larger than life on a large screen.

Disadvantages are the cost of the hardware, and the requirement of computing skill.

PRACTICAL SKILLS

Question: What personal techniques are displayed by the accomplished speaker?

The manner and skills of the good speaker are apparent at every stage of his or her presentation. The skills can be practised and learned:

First Impression
It is the moment of truth. The speaker is introduced. He or she stands up, or walks to a lectern or table. Wait. The first thing to do is to wait until there is silence. Usually, the nervous speaker pays little attention to the audience or the room. He or she is overcoming the very real hurdle of speaking. But the audience does not necessarily know of the speaker's personal fears and apprehensions. Outwardly they are disguised. It is essential that the speaker waits, in silence, with a confident smile until there is the attention of everyone. Some may be reading. Others at the back may be talking to each other.

The speaker has to have the attention of everyone. With a large audience, it may be appropriate to bang on a table. In a small audience, silence is all that is necessary. When attention has been gained, the speaker begins.

The author has seen many nervous speakers come to a lectern and read their own name and the title of their presentation from their notes. There is no excuse for that. The opening words must be memorised and rehearsed. That is all that is needed to grasp and hold the attention of everyone present.

Eye Contact
Despite the need to refer to notes, the speaker must look at the audience. This is an ongoing requirement. Looking into the eyes of the audience, from right to left and back again, has to be achieved. It is not enough to fix upon one person and talk to them.

Inexperienced speakers talk to the floor, to the ceiling, to their notes, or straight ahead.

The speaker must look at his audience

Posture

The ideal position is with feet apart, with the body well balanced. If there are no notes to hold, the hands should be lightly clasped on the stomach. Common faults are bending over to clutch the sides of a table, or in the case of men, standing with both hands in their pockets.

Ideally, hands are used for gestures that reinforce the words being spoken. But if hands are a problem to the inexperienced speaker and they seem to get in the way, holding notes may be the answer. When a flip chart or map is used during the presentation there is often a pointer. This is a pitfall for the unwary too. Many speakers play with the pointer as they are talking. They roll it, turn it, twist it, unaware that they are distracting the audience.

[41]

Voice Control

The voice, for the speaker, is a wonderful tool. It allows the speaker to grasp the attention of the audience and to hold it firmly, caressing and persuading. But the voice only exerts its influence when it is used effectively. The pitch must vary, and the speed of talking has to change. If not the voice tone becomes monotonous. It drones on. The audience is captive so if there is nothing to disturb in the warm relaxing room, the eyes begin to close. The audience dozes.

Hand in hand with the power of the voice is the strength of the absence of voice. Silence. A controlled pause easily breaks down audience barriers of inertia, hostility or disinterest. The way to gain audience interest and attention, when starting speaking, is through a strong opening. For this, a quotation or witty saying has been suggested. Equally effective is a short pithy statement followed by the controlled pause.

'Gentleman. I can solve your management problems!' followed by a pause of two to three seconds. During this time the speaker looks round confidently at the audience. Everyone waits to hear what is coming next.

Within voice control there are two common faults, unknown to the speakers themselves:

(1) **Mumbling.** The way to find out is to listen to a tape recording. Or ask a friend.

(2) **Dropping the voice at the end of a sentence.** When this happens the audience starts to fall asleep. The voice must be lifted at the end of the sentence to maintain vitality. Ask a friend to tell you if it happens.

Language Control

The language of a good presentation is concise, simple language. It is simple in structure. Both the sentence and the words used are short rather than long. They are pitched at a level the audience is going to understand. The speaker who speaks down to his audience is lost.

Jargon and acronyms are to be avoided: there may be people in the audience who do not understand what the initials or short names stand for. And as a general rule swearing is avoided too.

A LAST-MINUTE CHECK

Question: What is the best way of perfecting a presentation?

Self Help Checklist for Making a Presentation

- On reaching the lectern adopt a confident speaking posture with feet slightly apart, hands clasped in front.

- Wait for silence until attention from everyone is obtained.

- Memorise the opening.

- Set the tone of the presentation through a short strong opening.

- Provide a route map of the speech pathway to be followed.

- Make continuous eye contact with members of the audience, from side to side and back.

- Reinforce points with hand gestures.

- Speak slowly: use controlled pauses.

- Keep the voice up at the end of sentences.

- Remember eye contact all the time.

- Finish with a strong close.

SUMMARY

Question: What is the best way of preparing for a presentation?

Answer: A set of four rules structure the preparation for a presentation. They are:

(1) Identify the target audience

(2) List the key points

(3) Write out the speech in full

(4) Condense the speech to headings and trigger words: write these on postcard sized cards

Question: What is a practical format for a presentation?

Answer: Every presentation must have a beginning, a middle and an end. In the beginning section there is a linked series of steps:

(a) welcome

(b) self identification

(c) benefits

(d) route map

(e) style

In the middle section the steps are:

(1) set the scene

(2) identify the main problem

(3) consider the important options

(4) present the proposal

The close must be strong.

Question: What helps to turn an ordinary presentation into an excellent presentation?

Answer: The speaker in an excellent presentation is in control of his or her audience at all times. Quotations or witty sayings, researched in advance, are used to open strongly and to close.

Question: What visual aids are used to best effect?

Answer: Visual aids are used to reinforce a presentation and help understanding. Flip charts, overhead slides, 35 mm slides and computer graphics all provide visual reinforcement hand in hand with the spoken word.

Question: What personal techniques are displayed by the accomplished speaker?

Answer: The manner and skills of the accomplished speaker rest on immaculate first impressions, excellent ongoing eye contact, a relaxed confident posture, hand gestures, and full voice control that uses voice inflection and pauses. The language used by the accomplished speaker is pitched at exactly the level of the audience in short, uncomplicated sentences.

Question: What is the best way of perfecting a presentation?

Answer: A checklist covering all the main points to be observed is a very useful reminder for the person about to make a presentation.

4

AUDIO-VISUAL IMPACT

QUESTIONS

What factors influence a decision to use audio-visual resources?

What are the ingredients of an audio-visual event?

What high tech and graphics equipment enhance audio-visual presentations?

WHY AUDIO-VISUAL?

Question: What factors influence a decision to use audio-visual resources?

To the first time user, audio-visual resources appear very expensive. There is a sophisticated range of effects available in this medium, from slide/sound to professional film. Out of context, reference to £6,000 per second of finished production for a television commercial makes many businessmen blink. Managements often decide that they want to use something 'different', but are not really sure where to start.

So the starting point is identifying what is to be achieved by an audio-visual event:

- What is the prime objective? Is it to announce a new product? Is it to introduce change? Is it the intention to motivate a sales force; or simply to sell? The answer links to how the audio-visual event is able to meet the need.

- Who are the target audience? How many will be present? For example, the best viewing audience for a domestic size television screen is about thirty people. With a larger audience other equipment is more appropriate.

- What will the target audience do after the event, if all goes according to plan? Are staff needed to sell, administrate, take orders, or give advice?

- What venue is available? Is there appropriate equipment available or access for its installation? Is there likely to be distracting or competitive noise?

What will the target audience do after the event?

- Are the audio-visual resources to represent one component, out of a number of components, as back-up to an organised event? Or is the event to rest on the impact of a film or multi slide/sound show, as the main ingredient?

- Are the audio-visual effects to be achieved in-house, or through collaboration with professional companies?

- What is the budget available? A sophisticated show has to have a budget to match!

- Is the event to be a one-off event? Repeat events influence the choice of the audio-visual medium.

After the questions are asked and answered, the next step is to consider the spectrum of audio-visual resources.

NUTS AND BOLTS

Question: What are the ingredients of an audio-visual event?

There are two major ingredients for an audio-visual show – (1) slide and (2) film.

Slides
A simple slide programme uses 35 mm film slides with audio tape, through a single projector. It is easy to set up, to give a short presentation to small audiences. The standard slide projector gives a large single image up to 45 ft. wide. By using special equipment this size can be doubled without difficulty. As the standard equipment is compact and easily transportable it can be used in-house or at a customer's premises.

More sophisticated slide-tape programmes employ two or more projectors – up to about one hundred for very large events – with many screens. Most programmes use carousel type projectors linked to audio cassettes and 'dissolve' equipment. The sound effects and the picture quality are good.

An advantage of slide-tape programmes is that they are easy to change, if the material has to be updated. Costs are relatively low compared to film. For example, a two projector slide-tape programme costs from £500–£750 per minute of finished programme. For a six projector slide-tape programme the fee is likely to be double. A plus factor is that presentation equipment is widely available for hire. Another plus factor is that slide-tape programmes are easily transferred to video tape.

Film

Film is used in two forms – video tape and 16 mm film. Video tape is much less expensive than film but is subject to certain constraints. The tape cannot be edited, as with a film, which can be cut wherever required and spliced together again. Instead, a video tape is copied. Every time a video copy is made, known as a second generation tape, quality is lost. And the loss of quality in the form of blur and poor definition increases with third, fourth and successive generation tapes. The standard video tape is half-inch size and is played on *VHS (Video Home System)* equipment, *Betamax* or *VCR*. Because of the relatively low cost, and the ease of copying, video tapes are widely used.

Going up in the quality scale is *Low Band U-matic*. With a higher specification still, reaching to 'broadcast quality', the equipment is *High Band U-matic*. The tape size is one inch, using an open reel instead of cassette. The recording equipment is highly sophisticated and expensive.

To balance the benefits of high film quality against the cost of production, video tape is often shot on high band, and copied onto low band or VHS quality. Finished production costs per minute of tape using this method are currently £600–£900.

16 mm film is an excellent medium. The opportunities for visual impact and audience influence are boundless. But the production must be professional. People will not be impressed by home movies

when they are used to commercial film. To make use of film the budget must be large and unstinting. Otherwise, don't bother!

HIGH TECH PLUS

Question: What high tech and graphics equipment enhance audio-visual presentations?

There is a range of equipment, from the relatively simple prompter to the highly sophisticated video wall, designed to add effect to audio-visual events.

Teleprompter

Public speaking, for the inexperienced manager, is often a nightmare. One solution is in the form of a computerised prompt system. A magnified image of speech text, in large clear lettering, is displayed at eye level on one or two screens. To the audience the screens are totally clear and transparent. The sentences of the pre-written speech unroll slowly, geared to the speed of the speaker. The display pauses when the speaker pauses or increases tempo when the mood is lifted. When two screens are used, and placed one at each side of the audience, the speaker is forced to look from side to side across the audience. This is an excellent way of helping the speaker to maintain eye contact with his or her audience.

Speakers using the prompt no longer need to have notes or to memorise their words. A leading hire service company of prompting systems is Autocue Ltd., Autocue House, 265 Merton Road, London SW18 5JS; Telephone 01–870 0104; Fax 01–874 3726. Currently they quote £200–£300 daily hire charge.

Video Graphics

Sophisticated presentations combine photographic images and computer generated images in a single presentation. For example a company's new product, together with a photograph of the chairman, can be merged with a display of expected revenues and profits. And the presentation can last for seconds or many minutes, or can have composite still images printed on A4 size paper or overhead transparency film. With most systems up to seven colours are available for a single dot. So combinations of dots can form thousands of colour patterns.

The range of overall presentation effects is immense. It includes screen text highlighting, step by step picture building, moveable on-screen pointers, and all manner of dynamic attention-holding special effects.

Depending on what is required, the starting point for a comprehensive hardware and software package is about £10,000. An appropriate place to begin is discussing objectives and requirements with a dealer and service organisation. A small, rapidly growing company is Mass Mitec, The Warwick House, 38 Main Street, Lubenham, Market Harborough, Leicestershire LE16 9TF; Telephone 0858–410366.

Video Wall

Self stacking video screens, 28″ and 32″, have been developed to form a video wall. The system effect for the entertainment and information industries is highly dramatic. It has been used to operate against the dimness of a disco, or to grasp attention in a brightly lit exhibition hall. Equally, the system is used to advertise or inform at a sports stadium.

The images offered range from a single composite picture across the entire 'wall' of screens, to a combination of different images on each screen – Fig. 4.1. There is colour wash, moving image, or individual monitor freeze frames. The choice is a function of need, creative objectives, and budget.

A company supplying the multi-effect video wall is Cameron Video Systems Ltd., Burnfield Road, Giffnock, Glasgow G46 7TH, Scotland; Telephone 0041–633 0077 Fax 041–633 1745.

A figure has been quoted of approximately £8,000 for a 2 × 2 video wall. As with all video presentation activities, cost effectiveness stems from a system tailored exactly to client needs.

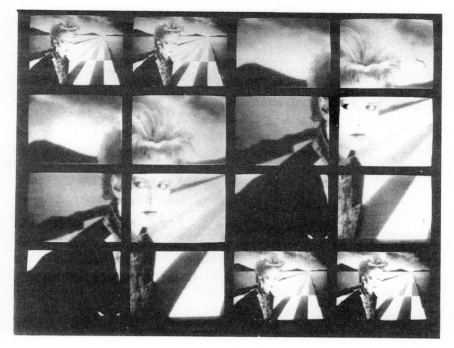

FIG.4.1   *Video Wall*

Talking to an expert, as opposed to buying do-it-yourself hardware and software, is a must.

SUMMARY

Question: What factors influence a decision to use audio-visual resources?

Answer: Before deciding to stage an audio-visual event it is essential to consider the following points:
    What is the event to achieve? Who are the target audience? What

must the audience do? Is the event to be one-off? What financial resources are available?

Question: What are the ingredients of an audio-visual event?

Answer: The most common ingredients of an audio-visual event are tape-slide show or film. Film is also widely available in video recording.

Question: What high tech and graphics equipment enhance audio-visual presentations?

Answer: The range of equipment ranges from the teleprompter, through sophisticated video graphics, to the bank of self stacking video screens integrating into a video wall.

5

PROFESSIONALISM ON
THE PHONE

QUESTIONS

What reactions other than irritation arise when a caller is subjected to a poor telephone manner?

What techniques are involved in answering a telephone efficiently?

How is a caller's level of expectation of good service on the phone raised?

What communication skills help selling on the phone?

What practical techniques are helpful in negotiating by phone?

ESSENTIALS

Question: What reactions other than irritation arise when a caller is subjected to a poor telephone manner?

The telephone is vital to a business. It is an essential communication link between supplier and customer, and within the company itself.

Usually it is taken for granted. The telephone and related activities intrude only when performance is not of an acceptably high standard.

A good telephone manner is made up of four major factors:

- Speaking clearly

- Courtesy

- Empathy

- Good communication

If the contribution of any of the factors is weak, awareness of the medium is heightened. The telephone changes from its role as an everyday communication tool to that of a constraint or threat. Poor telephone communication generates instant irritation. The threshold between irritation and frustration is invariably low. Anger follows.

GETTING IT RIGHT

Question: What techniques are involved in answering the phone efficiently?

The starting point in developing a business-like skill in answering the phone is analysis. The stages of the incoming call are identified. A technique is then formulated to structure the pattern of behaviour. The stages of the incoming call are:

(1) Behavioural reaction to the telephone ring.
The ring is a signal to action. The demand is heightened the longer the rings are allowed to continue. Three rings is a good number to set as a target at which to respond. Sometimes, for a variety of reasons, response time is extended.

The ring is a signal to action

With a single telephone receiver, the person answering the call should smile as the receiver is picked up. Smiling is infectious. It transmits through conversations. Smiling also relaxes the person smiling in small but perceptible measure.

On a busy switchboard the volume of calls does not always permit the pre-call smile. Comment has been made by participants on training courses, when asked to smile, that it is possible at 9.00 a.m. in the morning. At 4.30 p.m. on a busy day smiling is more difficult. For this reason positive effort has to be made each time the phone receiver is picked up. Smiling forms a habit pattern. It is productive.

Technique No. 1 Smile As You Pick Up the Receiver.

(2) Vocal statements.
'Hello' is a warm and friendly greeting. By itself it is inappropriate as an opening greeting to an answered telephone. The tone may be warm and friendly, but the response should be factual and informative.

The opening greeting at business premises differs depending on whether the person answering is taking an inside or outside call. With an inside call the name of the company is of course known. Exceptions to this statement are when one or more subsidiary companies are connected to the same switchboard. It is necessary for the responder to state his or her name, and where appropriate the department or section name.

With an outside call, the number and the company name, or the name by itself are used. Some companies instruct their switchboard operators to say 'Good Morning' or 'Good Afternoon' before giving the number. In this way interference on the telephone line, or a bad connection that sometimes occurs, does not delete any part of the number.

In any phone call there are two parties. The identity of the caller is important too. Psychologically many plus points are gained if the caller hears his name spoken by the person answering. It person-alises the call. The name should be requested and written down, together with the other essential notes needed as reference.

Technique No. 2 Answer by saying 'Good Morning' or 'Good Afternoon' and then giving your number or the name of your department to the caller.

Technique No. 3 Obtain caller's name.

(3) Interactive responses.
Action is taken or information given.

The language of the person answering a call should be crisp and business-like. Certain things are forbidden.

- Never eat, smoke or drink whilst talking on the phone.
- Do not mumble.
- Do not use jargon.
- Do not swear.
- Do not use long, complicated sentences.
- Do not leave callers hanging on in mid conversation for longer than ten seconds, without warning of the length of the delay.

Technique No. 4 Provide, or obtain and provide, the information or action requested.

[58]

Never eat, smoke or drink on the phone

(4) Conclusion of the call.

A busy caller has things to do. Chatting to an unknown person, or one of fleeting acquaintance, has low priority. The image created for the caller during the call is reinforced by the closing moments. Assertive, courteous control is business-like and effective: 'So that is the address to contact Mr. Brown. The local depot can certainly provide service when you need it. Thank you for calling. Goodbye.'

The sloppy call, discourtesy and rudeness are remembered vividly. The quietly professional response is not remembered in the same way, but the caller's expectation of good service is sustained, or if it is a first call, created at a high level.

When the call is a request for service back-up, the caller may want to make contact with the company again. Your name, or a contact name, should be given. Finding the right person in a large, anonymous company is time consuming and often daunting.

Technique No. 5 Close the call in a business-like manner, giving your name if subsequent contact is to be made.

PLANNING FOR A GOOD PUBLIC IMAGE

Question: How is a caller's level of expectation of good service on the phone raised?

When telephoning on business, the caller has a pre-set attitude. Historical experience of speaking to that number, or hearsay, influence the expectation of the level of response. And when the level of expectation is low, a poor response is unlikely to be tolerated easily.

Experimentally, in a training environment, it is easy to identify the behaviour that influences levels of expectation of service. It is also possible to predict the likelihood of levels of expectation rising or falling. So with training it is possible to plan for staff performance to generate a very high level of expectation of good service.

The training experiment is easy to conduct. Ten telephone call enquiries, for service or timetable information, are made and recorded on video tape. The target calls are to well known organisations, companies and institutions providing service to the public. Typical examples are:

British Rail

British Airways

Anglian Water Board

London Electricity Board

Everest Double Glazing Ltd.

Bristol Street Motors Ltd.

Kwik-fit Euro Exhausts Co. Ltd.

It is invariably found that with some calls the service is excellent. With others it is terrible.

At a training seminar participants are set an exercise. They are told that they are going to hear the taped recording of each of the telephone enquiries. Before each call participants are asked to write down, on a scale of zero to ten, their expectation of the level of service to be received. Appalling service is scored zero. Immaculate service is scored ten.

The calls are played. Participants are then asked to rate their level of expectation of service for their next call to the particular company.

Average results for this exercise, used frequently as a training resource, have shown:

- The level of expectation of service drops three points on a scale of ten after a single experience of bad service.

- The level of expectation of service climbs by one point on a scale of ten after an experience of good service.

When listening to the taped recording participants analyse the call into component factors. Fig. 5.1 illustrates a 'level of expectation grid'. Participants evaluate performance on the basis of

- **Reliability.** A caller perceiving reliability believes that whatever is promised is going to be carried out; whatever is stated is true.

- **Confidence.** The manner in which a call is answered structures the caller's perception. A strong, authoritative voice and the absence of indecision are indicators of confidence.

- **Helpfulness.** Helpfulness is a plus. Extra information and suggestions that go beyond the immediate limits of the

Level of Expectation rating 'before'	Call No.	Reliability	Confidence	Helpfulness	Efficiency	Personal Interest	Level of Expectation rating 'after'
	1						
	2						
	3						
	4						
	5						
	6						
	7						
	8						
	9						
	10						

Rate your level of expectation on a scale of 0–10. 10 is the highest expectation.

Place tick in appropriate space each time one of the listed qualities of service is perceived.

FIG. 5.1 *Level of Expectation Grid*

conversation or enquiry are a ready measure of willingness to assist.

- **Efficiency.** Efficiency is most readily identified in a negative way, by its absence. An efficient skill on the telephone is not intrusive. Examples of efficient behaviour are – identity stated, questions answered, and actions implemented without fuss or indecision.

- **Personal interest.** Even when the response is in the most general terms, personal interest raises the quality of the call. It is readily identifiable by awareness that the person answering cares.

As participants listen to the taped calls they place a tick in the grid each time one of the listed qualities is perceived. This helps build a picture of the effectiveness of the call. In a telephone call where there is expectation of good service, it is reinforced when all of the qualities are present. So a pathway to making the expectation of service high for all calls is identified. All personnel answering the phone must reflect the qualities discussed. The following checklist has applications:

Place a tick in appropriate square   YES   NO

- Did I smile when picking up the receiver?   ☐   ☐

- Did I respond as near as possible to the third ring?   ☐   ☐

- Did I answer with the phone number and my department
  or name?   ☐   ☐

- Did I help the caller positively?   ☐   ☐

- When waiting was unavoidable, did I offer the caller the
  choice of calling back or holding on?   ☐   ☐

	YES	NO
• When the caller was holding on did I keep him or her informed of the current situation, and of any further delays?	☐	☐
• Did I seek feedback from the caller that their needs were being met?	☐	☐
• When further contact with the company was necessary did I leave the caller with a contact name?	☐	☐

If the answer is YES, O.K. If NO, do something about it!

SELLING ON THE PHONE

Question: What communication skills help selling on the phone?

Communication is a set of skills. Selling is another. The two sets interweave. Selling on the phone is a planned activity where the seller leads the prospective customer along a projected path. At the end is the objective, the sale.

In effective selling, the prospective customer does not know that he or she is being led. Questions are asked and answered. Gradually the customer perceives that the benefits being offered are exactly right for what he or she wants. There is no overt pressure. And so a sale is closed.

Selling on the phone has two aspects: (1) planning and (2) performance.

Planning

The planning stage is in two parts.

(1) Identifying prospective customers.
Telephone contact should only be made with categories of customer from whom there is some chance of obtaining business. Divide the existing customer base into groups comprising the different types of

customer. For example, a pie manufacturer supplies hotels, restaurants, industrial caterers, British Rail and sporting event caterers. Names and addresses within these categories are available from trade directories, Yellow Pages, local newspapers, and by observation. Prospecting phone calls should be restricted, at least for an initial trial period, to these categories of customer.

(2) Designing the call.

Fig. 5.2 is a flow chart of the selling call. There is no chatting time available. Every moment on the phone must be used to effect. Possibly there is going to be hostility. The conversation has to be centred on issues most likely to be of interest to the customer. These are not necessarily known. So they must be guessed.

However successful or suitable the caller's products may be the prospective customer does not necessarily want to hear about them. In the successful sales call on the phone, the person called is involved right away. This helps to prevent immediate rejection.

'Hello, Mr. Deakin. We are YumYum Pies Ltd. Do you know us?' Whether or not the caller is known, this opening brings the prospective buyer into the conversation immediately. The follow-on response to the 'Yes' or the 'No' is prepared in advance. It describes succinctly the business of YumYum Pies Ltd.

It is essential for the caller to find out immediately the nature of the prospective customer's potential needs.

'Do you provide catering services to the new Deacon Industrial Estate?'

As soon as there is relevant information the caller goes for the prime objective close:

'Our bakery is three hundred yards from the Estate. We provide fresh daily deliveries, at competitive prices with no transport costs. When may we let you have sample pies to taste?'

The caller plans for the eventuality of the close failing. Credibility is sold to revive interest:

'Do you know that we supply Ring & Brymer Ltd. and Trust House Forte in comparable locations? In both cases their concern is with quality control and a competitive price. In our business additional

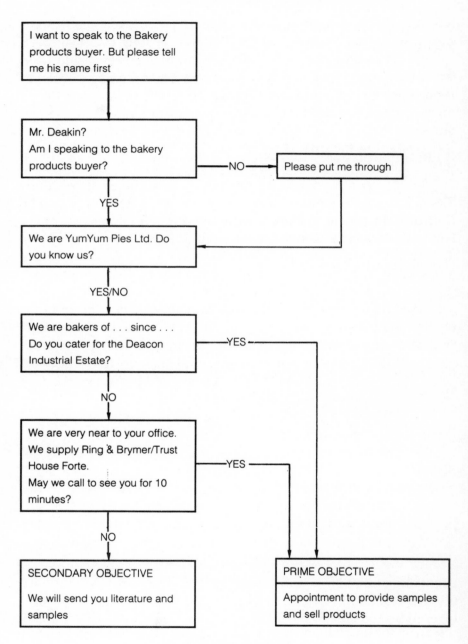

FIG. 5.2 *The Telephone Sales Call*

cost savings are available on the basis of seasonal menu changes. May we call. . . ?'

Performance

Successful selling on the phone obeys the following Golden Rules:

(1) Be authoritative.
The caller's voice reflects confidence and efficiency, but is without aggression

(2) Bring the person called into the conversation immediately.
For a sale to be achieved the conversation must be two-way.

(3) Ask probing questions.
The real needs of the person called must be established quickly. Without this knowledge opportunities for selling are limited

(4) Sell benefits.
Stress the advantages to the person called continuously.

(5) Treat 'No' as an objection to be overcome.
Successful selling has to overcome all objections. A question the caller should always consider before selling on the phone is: 'Do I want business, or do I want to be liked?'

TELEPHONE NEGOTIATIONS

Question: What practical techniques are helpful in negotiating by phone?

Negotiating is different to selling. Usually selling occurs within the negotiating function. Conceptually, in selling one party is fixed, the other is flexible. In negotiating, both parties are flexible, working together to see if a deal is possible.

Negotiating is a complex process demanding careful planning and preparation. But it is possible to negotiate without either. The brash negotiator says: 'I don't need to prepare. I'll see what they come up with, and react to that.' Negotiations do indeed then take place, because words are exchanged. But the negotiations are not as effective as they might have been with careful preparation. Poor negotiation loses profits, and misses out on concessions that could have been won.

For negotiating on the phone there are three important stages:

(1) Pre-discussion preparation

ME	THEM
• What are my objectives?	• What are the other side's objectives?
• What is my best possible position?	• What is their best position?
• What is the least position to permit a deal?	• What is their least position?
• What concessions do I want?	• What concessions do they want?
• What do these concessions cost me in money terms?	• What do their concessions cost them?
• What are these concessions worth in value terms?	• What are their concessions worth in value terms?
• What tactics do I use?	• What tactics are they likely to use?

In addition to preparing answers to the above questions it is important to identify the negotiating variables. In any business there are constants and variables. For example, with regard to product X the unit width is always 25 cms. It has always been so because that is the jig used. So it is a constant. The strength of product X is a variable because it is a function of the component chemical mix.

In terms of doing business there are variables and constants. Usually they are formed by historical precedent. Examples are payment terms, delivery time, specification, packaging, labelling, product colour, size, shape, weight. Pricing, quantities and tied purchasing are variables too.

In a negotiation, can a constant be changed to a variable, in exchange for concessions drawn from the other side? This is the homework that must precede negotiating on the phone.

(2) Sparring
The objective of this stage is to obtain information from the other side without giving anything material away.

Assumptions have been made about the other side. You have guessed their capacity, their demands, and their willingness to deal. You ask questions to test the assumptions. If you have been correct, you may be near to assessing the limits to which they will go. But hand in hand with the answers, or in place of them, direct leading questions are likely to be posed to you, to uncover information wanted by the other side. The more skilfully that you side-step the questions put to you, the stronger your negotiating position remains.

Rule of Thumb (a) **Probe to identify limits of other side's position.**

(b) **Answer questions with generalities.**

(c) **Respond to difficult direct questions by ignoring and asking own direct questions as the reply.**

(d) **Offer diversionary enquiries to deflect the nature of own precise needs.**

(3) Trading
In this final stage, bargaining takes place. Concessions are traded. For every concession that is granted, something is demanded in

return. On certain issues you know that you are unable to grant any concessions. In that case present them as a condition subject to which negotiations can proceed.

Rule of Thumb (a) Before granting concessions establish other side's total shopping list.

(b) Grant one composite concession to reflect all the other side's demands.

(c) Maintain printed list of your negotiating variables in sight throughout phone call.

SUMMARY

Question: What reactions other than irritation arise when a caller is subjected to a poor telephone manner?

Answer: A poor telephone manner is a constraint to business. It leads easily to irritation from which frustration and anger follow.

Question: What techniques are involved in answering a telephone efficiently?

Answer: There are five techniques for answering the telephone efficiently. They are:

Technique No. 1: Smile as you pick up the receiver.

No. 2: Answer by stating the number and your name or department to caller.

No. 3: Obtain caller's name.

No. 4: Provide, or obtain and provide, the information or action requested.

No. 5: Close the call in a business-like manner giving your name if subsequent contact is to be made.

Question: How is a caller's level of expectation of good service on the phone raised?

Answer: Staff using the phone are shown in a training session how a caller's level of expectation is influenced by performance. A self help checklist permits performance to be monitored.

Question: What communication skills help selling on the phone?

Answer: Selling on the phone has two aspects, (1) planning of the flow chart structure of the call and (2) performance, incorporating the golden rules of selling.

Question: What practical techniques are helpful in negotiating on the phone?

Answer: There are three important stages to negotiating on the phone:

(1) Pre-discussion preparation of the structure of the negotiation and the variables to be used.

(2) Sparring to test hypotheses of other side's position, with rule of thumb guidelines to behaviour.

(3) Trading of concessions with further rule of thumb guidelines to the bargaining process.

6

PUBLIC RELATIONS

QUESTIONS

What is PR?

What kind of public image does a company want to have?

What public image does the company have now?

Who should PR activities reach?

What format should the PR message take?

What practical PR event is manageable without professional help?

A DEFINITION

Question: What is PR?

PR is public relations. It is how others think of a company or person or committee or activity. Companies have images. Any one company will have as many images as there are people who think about it. Fig. 6.1 illustrates the different public images of a manufacturing

FIG. 6.1 *The Different Public Images of a Manufacturing Company*

company. The company's customers, potential customers, bankers, the firm's staff, the competitors, distributors, suppliers, the trade association, and the trade sector's consumer movement all have a view.

Ideally, all should think well of the company. So one of a company's set objectives should be to generate good public relations.

'ABC Taxis Ltd.? Oh yes, they are always reliable.' 'Zenith Fashions Plc.? I am most impressed. Each year they offer better and better designs.'

PR does not go away if it is ignored. The different publics still have their view even if a company takes no particular steps to enhance its image. Provided mishaps, such as failed appointments, incorrect deliveries, late payment, or even simple lack of courtesy are not excessive, business continues. But when energies are specifically directed at creating and maintaining a good public image, the story is very different. Satisfied customers, aware of the benefits of the products or services that they buy, are the stepping stones to growth.

THE IDEAL IMAGE

Question: What kind of public image does a company want to have?

There are many ways of thinking about a company. 'It is helpful. It is innovative. The company looks after its staff well. The product range is excellent. Deliveries are always on time.'

The first task for a company concerned with its image is to identify how it wants to be seen by its publics. A brainstorming session by senior management is a good way of providing this information.

Effective brainstorming has a leader to conduct the session. First the leader produces a 'nonsense' item. It might be a length of twisted plastic tubing, a broken bottle sliver, a piece of stone – anything that does not have an immediate structured relationship to the brainstorming group. The leader asks the group to say in how many different ways the 'nonsense' object can be used. He pushes the group to shout out ideas. The leader stresses that constraints of propriety, for the purpose of the exercise, be removed. The objective is to warm up the group in preparation for the brainstorming task to follow. If the leader is good at encouraging his group the ideas produced become more and more outlandish. Concepts begin to cross traditional sexual, social, or medical boundaries. After about twenty minutes, the group is ready to address the problem in hand.

Every idea produced by the members of the group on how the company should be seen by others is then recorded. A flip chart is useful. When the ideas stop flowing, the leader moves on to the next brainstorming stage. The items are grouped in order of importance or effectiveness. A reverse brainstorming session is then conducted for those items at the top of the list: this is to screen out the non-runners. The leader, taking each item in turn, pushes his group to consider in how many ways the selected item is inappropriate or unsuitable.

By the end of the session the group is in a position to identify clearly how it wishes to be seen by all of its publics. Then, after finding out what the present public image is, PR objectives can be set, providing targets to be reached.

Linked to the public image is the **position** of the company in the market place. This is most important too. Fig. 6.2 illustrates the position of a food manufacturing company that is seen as modern/innovative and up-market. In marketing terms a company is identified by the market segment in which it trades. A segment is that grouping within the market place within which all the buyers have identical needs. Lager drinkers are a segment of the market. So are families with two children. Other examples are teenagers who wear jeans, or snack food eaters.

Within a segment there are many positions a company takes, but always at a point between two polar opposites. For example, a company may be described as dominant or anonymous, young or old and established, or anywhere between the two extremes. The very small company does not really have a significant position in the market place. But with growth, management should decide what the best position should be. It is, in effect, the real identity of the firm. In marketing terms, position is a measure of achievements and strengths.

WHO ARE WE?

Question: What public image does the company have now?

A necessary step towards creating a good public image is finding out what the image is at present. Professional public relations consultants can do this for you, for a fee. A useful contact source is:

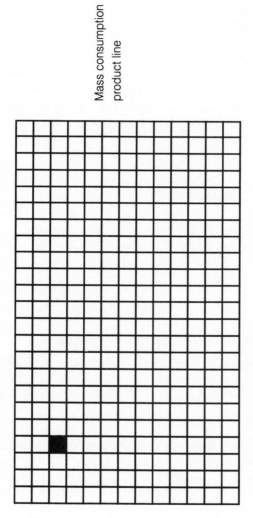

Modern/Innovative

Up-market
product line

Old fashioned/Traditional

Mass consumption
product line

FIG. 6.2 *Position of Food Manufacturing Company within Industry Sector*

Public Relations Consultants Association
Premier House, 10 Greycoat Place
London SW10

Tel: 01–222 8866

But finding out can be done in-house, too, by mounting an image audit, addressed to the major different publics of the company. For credibility, the audit should be carried out by a senior manager or director, talking face to face to his or her counterpart.

Format For A Public Image Audit

'Thank you for agreeing to this meeting. We are researching to identify the present image of the company. May I please have your answers to a few questions? It would be helpful if the answers are all rated from bad to good on a scale of one to five: one is very bad. Five is very good.

- What is the quality/originality of our merchandise?
- What is the quality/originality of competitors' merchandise?
- What is the quality of our back-up service?
- What is the quality of our competitors' back-up service?
- How effectively do we demonstrate that we care for your particular needs?
- How effectively does the company communicate with you?
- How efficient are our personnel in their transactions with you?
- How competitive are our prices?
- How well are market trends reflected in our product range?
- How do you perceive the resources of our company?

- How do you perceive the track record of the company?

- What is the quality of the management of the company?

- How do you rate our company's efforts to publicise itself?

- How do you rate our company's efforts to publicise its products?

- What do you consider to be the company's prospects for growth: – in the short term – in the medium term?

- How do you rate the quality of our marketing?

- How reliable are our deliveries?

Thank you for those answers. One last question please: what do you consider are the company's strengths and weaknesses?'

TARGETING

Question: Who should PR activities reach?

Management has to work out what it wants to achieve through PR. The image audit tells where the company is. And management knows, because it has thought about it, where it would like to be. So objectives are set.

A common PR objective is to increase awareness of the company product. 'The "Holdit Household Clamp" has many different uses in the home.'

Another objective is to differentiate the company's services from others. 'Countem and Co. Chartered Accountants can help in Preparing Business Plans and Writing Procedures Manuals as well as with traditional accounting matters.'

Other objectives might be to persuade the public to buy company products, or to advise customers of better facilities. To meet the different objectives, questions have to be asked.

● *Who do we target for PR effort?*

There are many audiences. There are potential customers. Existing customers. Customers who have lapsed. Competitors' customers. Dissatisfied customers. There is the general public at large. There are the company's own employees. And does it matter if the competition itself is targeted?

The related question to ask is 'which audience is likely to react most favourably'. Two theories try to explain how PR works.

Theory 1 says that personal attitudes are changed by a PR campaign. If there is reference to a company or a product in print then it must be good. The printed word has authority. Advertisements have this authority too, but editorials and news items have it to a greater extent. And the impulse to buy the product, or be associated with the company, is created because of that authority.

Who do we target for PR effort?

Theory 2 says that post purchase doubts are extinguished. After making a purchase niggling doubts arise, particularly with goods or services of high capital value. 'Should I have done that? Can I really afford it?' Reading in the press about the product or service that has been bought is comforting. The reader feels warm all over. 'Oh yes. I made the right decision. Look, there it is. I bought that.' And there is a ripple effect spreading out through the purchaser's peer group. Everyone learns what a good thing it is to buy and have.

Whichever of the theories is the right one is not clear-cut. Perhaps it is a combination of both. So identifying the audience likely to react most favourably must rest on experience and judgement.

● *How do we reach the audience?*
The important media are the press, radio and television. But then further decisions are needed. Which is appropriate? With press, for example, there is local, regional, national, weekly or trade press. Which has the most cover? Which is the easiest to penetrate? Which has the widest or largest customer concentration? Local and regional newspapers make up the largest medium in the United Kingdom. And that applies both to numbers sold and to advertising revenue. Much of local press covers local business.

'High-tech comes to Little Haymarsh In The Wold. New electronic equipment installed at Higgins and Co means that tractors can now be repaired in half the time. . .'

Locating the local press should provide few problems. But to consider reaching an audience in other ways a press directory is essential. A press directory tells what papers, magazines, television and radio stations there are. It gives contact names, addresses, telephone numbers and what the speciality is.

Two useful directories are:

British Rate & Data   76 Oxford Street, London W1N 9FD
                       Tel: 01–434 2233
Willings Press Guide   Thomas Skinner Directories, Windsor Court,
                       Grinstead House, East Grinstead, RH19 1XE
                       Tel: 0342 26972

If neither meet every need, the librarian in the local library reference section can recommend others.

When making contact, the business editor, features editor, diary editor or perhaps the women's page editor is the starting point. Aiming at the top and contacting the editor is unlikely to offer advantage. A direct parallel is the starting point for selling paper clips to a new company. The office manager or the stationery buyer are best approached, not the managing director.

BEING NEWSWORTHY

Question: What format should the PR message take?

Newsworthy items mean information that is likely to interest readers – or listeners or viewers.

'Peter Piper Ltd has doubled its profits this year.' By itself this information is primarily of interest only to Peter Piper employees and shareholders.

'Peter Piper Ltd has doubled its profits this year and has to increase its workforce within the next three months, to maintain performance.' This item is newsworthy. The principle is the same as in selling a product benefit. What the benefit *does* for the buyer is described, not the intrinsic qualities of the product.

As a general statement, the section editor is always receptive to newsworthy items, from whatever source. But the editor's perception of what is newsworthy may not always coincide with the opinion of those making contact. PR items are always welcome. A formal introduction is not essential. Telephone contact may be made, or a 'press release' sent in the post. Telephone callers should not be discouraged if initial contact is difficult. Editors are busy people.

For the do-it-yourself PR person, writing copy to send to the press is not always easy. There are important rules:

(1) Try to emulate the style of the paper or journal. Read the style carefully. Compare it with other features, published elsewhere. What are the similarities? What are the differences?

(2) Keep it short.

(3) Answer the questions 'What? Where? Who? How? and When?'

(4) Provide your name, address, and contact phone number.

(5) State whether the item is for immediate release, or if not, for when.

(6) Write on white A4 size paper in double spacing leaving wide margins at the top, bottom and sides.

(7) Provide photographs when possible.

PR IN ACTION

Question: What practical PR event is manageable without professional help?

An excellent PR activity to stimulate business is an Open Day. But it demands careful planning and administration:

Open Day

The starting point is with the answers to the following questions:

- What do we want to achieve from the event?

- Who do we want to invite?

- How do we identify the names of companies and persons to whom to send invitations?

- What press coverage do we want?

- How long should the event last? When? And where?

- What is to be provided for the guests to see or do?

- Who is responsible for co-ordinating the event? (This is a must.)

- Who is to help: (a) with preparation (b) at the event (c) with ancillary activities to the event, i.e. reception, catering, parking, directions, cloakroom?

- What company resources/activities are to be displayed?

- Who is responsible for post event action?

- What training and rehearsal must be carried out?

Visitors to an event come for two main reasons: (1) to find out what is available generally or (2) for a specific purpose. This may be to place an order; it may be to obtain specific information, or to set in motion a particular action.

There is a third category. That is simply to pass the time – a day out – or to have a free lunch. No one admits to sinning in this way, but it does happen.

All events should have a theme. This helps particularly in the targeting of those to be invited. For a management centre selling a wide range of training skills, finding a theme is easy. It might be 'practical communication skills for businessmen' or 'marketing for the professions'.

It is equally possible for a food manufacturer of, say, chilled foods to find a theme. Where the product range is narrow, and the company sales activities are well established, careful thought is necessary to identify a fresh perspective. The event must have an edge that distinguishes it from an ordinary sales meeting. The food manufacturer might link an occasion such as an extension to the plant, or a visit from a Trade Association dignitary with an opportunity for existing and potential customers to visit the factory. A particular new benefit is identified for the visitors, as a theme. Naturally the press are invited.

A letter or leaflet describing the Open Day event is sent to all who are to be invited. A reply slip or card is attached. Those who do not reply within the stipulated time are telephoned. It is useful to identify in advance the area of interest for each visitor, so that when visitors arrive on the day, staff have been allocated to help them.

A reception desk is advisable, to make sure that the name and company details of each visitor are recorded.

Open days are enhanced by coffee, drinks, or buffet lunch. The extent of the catering is a matter of judgement. But when lunch is scheduled, the majority of visitors tend to cluster around mid-day. Visitors value the opportunity at this time to talk to acquaintances within the industry, who are also present.

When the Open Day is over, marketing and administration still carry on. All new leads and enquiries are entered into the customer data base. Orders received must be put in hand, and customer enquiries followed through.

The format of the Open Day should provide visitors with activities to see. Whenever possible there should be something for them to do too – tasting, weighing, evaluating, operating, judging, discussing or writing. And when visitors leave there should be something for them to take away – literature, business samples or gifts.

The effectiveness of the Open Day as a PR tool is evaluated when visitors have left. It is important to have an immediate discussion with all staff who participated, whilst impressions are vivid. Final analysis often has to wait until all pertinent data has been collated. At that point the following questions are asked:

- What is the total cost (inclusive of management and staff time, literature, mailing, office administration, catering, equipment hire)?
- What orders have been taken?
- What enquiries have been received?
- What future opportunities are identified?

- What proportion of contacts responded to the invitation?

- What trends are identifiable in respect of those attending (type of customer, geographical distribution, preferred time of visit, length of stay, interest in future open days)?

- What proportion of press invitations were accepted?

- What press exposure resulted?

- What is the staff reaction to the Open Day?

SUMMARY

Question: What is PR?

Answer: PR is public relations. It is how others think of a company or person or committee or activity.

Question: What kind of image does a company want to have?

Answer: A company should consider carefully how it wants to be seen by others. The desired position of the company within its market segment is relevant. Companies should decide on the image wanted and then set image objectives to structure their PR activities.

Question: What public image does the company have now?

Answer: A company has as many public images in the market place as there are companies, individuals or organisations with which it interacts. An image audit conducted by senior management helps to identify how others see the company.

Question: Who should PR activities reach?

Answer: First the target audience is decided – existing, lapsed or potential customers. Contact is then sought with the media providing the largest or widest audience concentration.

Question: What format should the PR message take?

Answer: For the do-it-yourself PR consultant there is a short set of rules structuring the press release to help match the media style. The most important rule is that the press release should answer the questions what? where? who? how? and when?

Question: What practical PR event is manageable without professional help?

Answer: An 'At Home' day for a company is an opportunity for old, new and potential customers, and for the media to visit the company. The day should be structured to provide visitors with information, maintain their interest, and motivate business. At the same time media coverage is sought.

7

DEALING WITH COLLEAGUES

QUESTIONS

What is the basis of good listening?

What training exercises are able to improve listening skills?

Why is assertiveness important to a manager or executive?

What actions help to increase assertiveness?

What techniques help to overcome aggression from others?

LEARNING TO LISTEN

Question: What is the basis of good listening?

Communication is a two-way process. It involves senders and receivers. Senders transmit messages and signals. For communication to take place those messages or signals must be received. At a face to face meeting both messages and signals are sent. Messages are conveyed in the form of words; signals are given by gesture and by posture.

But not every spoken word is heard. Listening is a skill. It is an active skill. The difference between hearing and listening is one of control: hearing is undifferentiated. When hearing is actively directed at and concentrated on a sound source it becomes listening. Few managers or executives have formal training to enhance their listening skills. The result is that much of what is said is heard but not retained. So problems arise from lack of retained information.

Example: A manager tells his department the new arrangements for access to the enlarged company car park. One of the arrangements is access restriction on a certain day. He announces the long-awaited opening of the new company canteen. He then dwells on successful departmental performance.

A number of the department members subsequently forget about the access restriction. They had heard, but did not listen to and retain, some of the boring instructions.

Communication breakdown due to poor listening occurs most frequently when the communicated message is long. Breakdown in communication for short messages is usually more a result of poor sending skills than poor receiving skills.

A person thinks far more quickly than he or she speaks. As a result, when listening to someone speaking, attention wanders for a number of reasons:

- the listener compares what is being said to incidents within his or her own experience and dwells on the latter,

- the listener races ahead to predict what the speaker may say. This is a mental sidetrack from which strength is needed to bring the listener back. Sometimes, at the return point the listener is lost. Pertinent data given by the speaker has not been absorbed. The listener then jumps back to the security of his or her own mental sidetrack journey.

- the listener competes with what he or she is hearing by calling up more satisfying examples.

Communication breakdown due to poor listening occurs most frequently when the communication message is too long

- the listener shuts out what is being said. This is in order to concentrate on preparing his or her own statements that are going to be spoken as soon as the opportunity arises.

- the listener mentally argues against what has been heard.

- the listener shuts off and daydreams.

These distractions are all self originating. Other distractions may be caused by the sender who is particularly handsome, or perhaps oddly dressed. Or a colleague might say something, or Concorde fly overhead.

Good listening can be compared to good running – another physical skill. For the athlete, good running is a concentrated effort to produce a given rhythm. To win races the athlete must train. The runner has to produce an output of physical exertion economically balanced against the human resources of stamina and physical fitness. And overall a structure appropriate to racing is imposed, allowing performance to reach a peak at a required point.

Listening is no different. Listening is improved by training. It permits the person who is listening to recall all the important messages given, and preferably the unimportant ones too. The listener has to develop the mechanism of not being distracted by boring, irrelevant or emotive information. A very real problem is that not all managers speak well. As the speaker searches for a way of expressing his or her understanding, the level of grammar drops: sentences become long and complicated.

Managers particularly have to listen well. It is an essential part of their job. More of a manager's day is spent in listening than in speaking or observing or writing or reading. Good listening encompasses:

- Concentrating on what is being said.

- Sifting out the essential meaning of what is said from irrelevant word flow.

- Interpreting gestures and facial expressions that reinforce or deny the speaker's statements.

- Resisting one's own emotional reaction to what is being said.

- Resisting the temptation to ignore opinions with which there is disagreement.

- Demonstrating to the speaker, by posture or facial expression, that what is being said is of interest.

PRACTICE MAKES PERFECT

Question: What training exercises are able to improve listening skills?

The most important aspect of training in listening skills is concentration on the act of listening. When a mental listening switch is switched on, hearing becomes listening.

Training is simple. One particularly successful exercise is in three parts. Working in pairs or small syndicates, one person reads a page of text to the partner, or to the others. Preliminary instructions are for the participants to listen carefully. Participants are tested on the extent of their recall. Differences in recall successes are discussed to identify different types of listening skill.

The exercise is continued with a different person reading. This time instructions are given for recall to be structured in respect of a particular aspect occurring within the text. Again recall successes are discussed, evaluating the advantages and disadvantages of directional listening.

For the third part of the training exercise participants work together in the same syndicates. Their task is to prepare a checklist on *how to listen effectively*.

If the training is in a classroom there is value in each syndicate presenting their checklist to the assembled group. In this way participants can take note of any checklist items prepared by others that are of personal use.

The real value of the checklist is the introspective search for the mechanism of listening. The listener becomes aware of the importance of concentration. And regular reference to the checklist defends against the intrusion of sloppy listening habits.

BEING ASSERTIVE

Question: Why is assertiveness important to a manager or executive?

Assertiveness is standing up for one's rights. So is aggression. But aggression is not concerned with how others feel. Assertiveness, in contrast to aggression, does not abuse or violate the rights of others. Consider the following example of a person living in London who changes his job.

The person is appointed to the post of factory manager at a factory in Liverpool. The position is from September 1st. The present London employment terminates on August 31st.

An assertive person travels up to Liverpool on September 1st. He does not want to travel in his own time because, in the circumstances, there is considerable time pressure and inconvenience.

The non-assertive or submissive person travels up to Liverpool, notwithstanding the personal difficulties and shortage of time, on the evening of August 31st. He wants to make a good impression in the new job by starting first thing.

The example is from real life. The job, many years ago, was the first managerial post for the person concerned. He decided that, in the circumstances, he was within his rights to travel up to the factory on September 1st when employment actually commenced. And this assertiveness was not cushioned by years of skill and experience. It was simply his attitude. Currently that manager is now a peer of the realm, and the chief executive of a very large organisation.

Being assertive has to impinge on the behaviour of others. Standing up for what you consider to be your rights brings you in conflict with others, who may not consider that your action is justified. Sadly, being assertive is not always a direct route to being liked. But the alternative – submissive behaviour – leaves you at the mercy of other people's actions.

Submissive behaviour gives in to the wishes of others. 'Would you mind staying after work tonight, until 9.00? Jenkins has promised to ring in as soon as he arrives in Milan.'

Submissive behaviour says 'yes', irrespective of any personal arrangements already made. In the short term it gets a person liked. Also, it is easier than arguing or causing displeasure. But in the long term, submissive behaviour is counter-productive to the desired end. Instead of making a person liked, it generates contempt and lack of respect. In management terms, a submissive manager is a non-starter.

The short term effects of aggressive behaviour towards others are often positive. Objectives are reached because all people standing in the way are swept aside; particularly if they have not met such dominant behaviour before. But aggressive behaviour over a longer period generates resistance and reaction. An aggressive manager faces absenteeism, low morale, lack of initiative, or lateness. Not everyone says openly, 'I cannot stand your lack of feeling, or the way you humiliate everyone.' They just leave.

Assertive behaviour is the most effective path for the manager between submission and aggression. It ensures that personal objectives can be reached, notwithstanding the people-hurdles that are always there. But there is a wide range of behaviour open to the assertive manager. Charm and skill with words go a long way to taking the sting out of assertive strength.

'No, Thomas, I must insist that you stay behind to finish this today. I know it is difficult for you with the arrangements that you have made: and I am sorry for this. But it has to be.'

TAKING THE INITIATIVE

Question: What actions help to increase assertiveness?

Assertive behaviour is not behaviour that is different in kind. It is an attitude making appropriate use of a number of everyday activities.

Asking for action

'Would you please get me the Blacker balance sheet.'

'On your way back please call and see if the deliveries have arrived.'

'Gentlemen. I want a full report on my desk by 9.00 a.m. tomorrow.'

A person who is not very assertive finds many good reasons for not asking.

– possible refusal with an argument to follow
– I haven't the right to ask
– he or she won't like it
– I may be ridiculed

Action: Plan three assertive requests over the next three days. Make them confidently. Do not apologise profusely, or justify. Nor should you 'sell' the request. Monitor the effect. If it is refused, well – others may have the right not to comply. But assertiveness achieves what submissive behaviour can never achieve. Planning and succeeding is always a great boost to confidence. So by planning to adopt a more assertive approach generally, every successful assertion is going to reinforce the assertive style.

Plan three assertive requests over the next three days

Refusing

'No' I'd rather not. . .'
'No. I am sorry, I prefer not to. . .'
Similar short, pointed statements, courteously and firmly given, are assertive refusal statements.

Refusing by giving real or invented excuses is submissive behaviour. Assertive behaviour is refusing because you do not want to do something, or you feel that it is not right that it should be done.

Refusing is harder than saying 'yes'. Thoughts occur such as 'The person asking may be offended' or 'He or she may not like me.' Another worry is 'The person asking is more important than me.'

Action: Plan the next three refusals that you are going to make. They are going to be three assertive refusals so that you can monitor the effect. How are you going to feel afterwards? What happens when you behave assertively?

Make sure that the refusal is short and authoritative, but without profuse apologies. If reasons are given, make sure that they are not offered as excuses to hide the fact of your making a refusal.

Criticising

'That's not right!'
'Your assessment of the depot's requirements is totally wrong.'
'Your performance this afternoon is simply not good enough.'
If criticism is made it may be accepted. More frequently criticism is resented, or rejected, or ridiculed, or a combination of all three. Criticism is often interpreted as an attack, so a counter attack is launched. Assertive criticism makes a statement that something is not up to a required standard. But the person criticised for a particular activity perceives a wider criticism embracing his or her overall competence. And this is very damaging to the ego.

Care should be taken that specific criticism is not open to interpretation as blanket criticism of the person concerned.

Action:

- Make it clear that the criticism is your personal criticism.
  'In my opinion your assessment of the situation is incomplete.'

- Make a specific criticism in preference to general criticism.
  Statements such as 'The finishing stage is not up to standard,' or
  'Your workbench is too untidy,' are more effective than 'I think
  your work is sloppy.'

- Link the criticism to a response invitation.
  'Do you realise that the sizes are different to the customer's
  order?' or 'The composition is wrong: why do you think that has
  happened?'

- Avoid personal attack.
  Do not make statements like 'You are an incompetent fool.'

- Link the criticism to a request for a remedy.
  'The left sleeve looks to be longer than the right. How can that be
  rectified?'

Praising

People like to be praised. Praise is a much under-used management
tool. Newly appointed managers often feel that their prime responsibility is to correct inadequate performance in their staff. So they go
and look for instances to correct. A far more effective approach is to
motivate staff to perform well.

Praise is an excellent means of achieving this end. The mechanism
is simple. Praise someone for the performance of an everyday task.
Management praise for routine activities that are taken for granted
is well received.

Assertive praise makes a positive statement. Provided that it is
given without overt embarrassment or condescension it reinforces
the authority of the person giving the praise.

Action: Identify a number of routine tasks for which to praise different members of staff – good timekeeping, a tidy desk, an efficiently documented store cupboard.

Use short, clear statements. 'Well done. That's an excellent effort.' Be sure to maintain good eye contact. Whenever possible give praise in front of others so that the person praised knows that others are aware.

DEALING WITH BULLIES

Question: What techniques help to overcome aggression from others?

Aggression has different forms. At one end of the scale is the physically belligerent person spoiling for a fight. 'Why the hell did you do that?' or 'Who is the idiot who left his car in the parkway?' Handling this aggression is helped by the warning signals flashing continuously. The aggressive person usually has a lot of momentum. One carefully worded soothing phrase is unlikely to defuse the stored energy. There are at least two issues. The person considers that something is not right. The person is aggrieved. The person may also feel that he or she is a victim of circumstances orchestrated by others.

There are three behavioural options for dealing with the belligerent bully – counter-aggression, submission, assertive behaviour.

Counter-aggression. A verbal battle marshalling bigger and better abuse is unlikely to resolve conflict. Worse – both sides finish in a state of tension, where initially only the aggressor had strong feelings, difficult to contain. A physical battle is an option but unrealistic. Fisticuffs do from time to time occur, but the final round has a chance of taking place in the Courts.

Submission. Non-assertive people submit when exposed to

strength in others. Occasionally assertive people submit too because of a combination of special factors. But the submissive act is followed by self recrimination. 'If only I had said . . .'. 'Why did I allow him to take control?' Submission in the face of aggression does nothing to diminish that aggression. Rather it reinforces and encourages further aggression.

Assertiveness. Assertive behaviour can be effective against aggression, provided that the assertive person makes the aggressor play by his or her rules. Assertiveness is only a viable force when personal rights are being upheld. This imposes limitations. A person assertive about everything is really an aggressor.

Action

Make the point of spoken contact with the aggressor an issue on which you feel strongly.

'Whatever your feelings about the delivery schedule, do not use swear words in this office. I will not have swearing in front of the other staff.'

Irrespective of the ranting of the aggressor, force the points of discussion to follow your own lead. The starting point is compliance with a pre-condition – no swearing, no smoking, reference to an original document or whatever is appropriate. The next point is the introduction of an issue which the aggressor is put in the position of defending or justifying.

A likely counter by the aggressor is to ignore the issue, pursuing one of his own, with or without more bad language. But the assertive person persists, staying firmly with his or her own topics.

At the other end of the aggression scale are sarcastic and sneering comments. 'Huh. Typical of you accountants' or 'How much longer do you need to get the stamps?'

The comments are often unexpected, and invariably unjustified. They vary in the strength of their barb and hurt.

There are three possible responses.

(1) Give like for like. If your wit is strong and you think quickly on your feet, putting down the person who started the exchange is very satisfying.

(2) Ignore the comments. This is a calculated unassertive option, but if the attack is only slight, it is economic husbandry of emotional resources.

(3) Treat the statements seriously and assertively.
'Oh. Hurry Up. Why don't you take some lessons in book keeping.'
The reply is 'You must wait. My system is the best for this office.'

SUMMARY

Question: What is the basis of good listening?

Answer: Listening is controlled directed hearing. Concentration is very important to sift out essential meaning and discard irrelevant word flow. When body language is visually available it must be interpreted to reinforce the listening effectiveness.

Question: What training exercises are able to improve listening skills?

Answer: A practical exercise has the following format. Participants listen to a passage of text, measure the extent of recall and then evaluate their performance. Subsequent preparation of a checklist, *How to Listen Effectively* is then helpful in reinforcing participant awareness of their personal listening skills.

Question: Why is assertiveness important to a manager or executive?

Answer: Assertiveness is standing up for one's rights. It is a balanced pathway between the extremes of submissive behaviour and aggression. Submission and aggression generally offer only short term advantage, if any.

Question: What actions help to increase assertiveness?

Answer: Assertiveness, making use of everyday activities, is put into practice through (a) asking for action (b) refusing (c) criticising and (d) praising.

Question: What techniques help to overcome aggression from others?

Answer: Aggression ranges from extreme belligerence to the one-off sarcastic or sneering remark.

Belligerent aggression must be handled assertively by dealing with specific issues and topics. The aggressor is forced to narrow the points of dialogue to those in which the assertive person is strong.

Sarcastic and contemptuous remarks are dealt with either by like for like conflict, or assertively. A third calculated option is to ignore the remarks.

8

CONDUCTING MEETINGS

QUESTIONS

Why are different meetings different?

What documentation is necessary for conducting meetings?

What pitfalls does a committee chairman encounter?

What format ensures a good meeting?

What are the principal formal aspects of a meeting?

OPTIONS

Question: Why are different meetings different?

Two or more people talking together can say they are having a meeting. But if they are together to achieve a particular purpose, that objective structures the meeting. There are different kinds of meetings. See Fig. 8.1.

Advisory Meetings. An advisory meeting is called to advise others. The purpose is to impart information. A problem may be identified,

CHOICE OF MEETINGS

FIG. 8.1   *Choice of Meetings*

and a solution sought and found. But obtaining feedback from those attending the meeting is not the function of an advisory meeting. Example: New undergraduates are invited to attend an advisory meeting to be informed of their dormitory arrangements.

Bargaining Meeting. This meeting is convened to reach a decision between two (or more) parties. The meeting provides an opportunity for the parties to present their case and negotiate a settlement. Example: Management and trade union meet to discuss and resolve payment of overtime rates.

Collegiate Meeting. Such meetings are attended by individuals of similar status who have an interest in the situation. There may be no formal chairman. Members contribute and exchange information, knowledge and ideas. Example: School teachers' common room meeting to discuss the arrangements for an informal Christmas party.

Command Meeting. The convenor of this meeting wishes to instruct others to carry out a plan of activity. Example: Parents of the bride and the vicar arrange a command meeting with the ushers, best man, bride and groom to lay down procedures for the forthcoming wedding.

Committee Meeting. This meeting is attended by two or more interest groups. A chairman is elected. Decisions are reached (in principle) on the basis of voting. Example: A meeting is called by the marketing manager, to discuss a projected trade exhibition in Dubai. The accountant, export manager, transport manager and production manager are invited to attend.

Company Meeting. There are two main categories – 'general' and 'special'. Legislation demands that general meetings are held annually, hence the name Annual General Meeting. This meeting includes (1) Chairman's Report (2) Accounts (3) Resolutions. Societies and organisations have an AGM as well as business companies.

A 'special' meeting is called to deal with one or more specific topics.

THE WRITING PART

Question: What documentation is necessary for conducting meetings?

Writing tasks start well before the day of the meeting. Notice of the meeting and the agenda are to be circulated by the secretary to all who must attend. If a secretary has not formally been appointed to the committee, the chairman takes responsibility for convening the meeting.

The wording of the notice is simple and straightforward.

PRODUCTION COMMITTEE

A meeting will be held in the Drawing Office on Tuesday 14th December at 9.00 a.m. to consider replacement equipment. An agenda is attached.

Please inform the Secretary if you are unable to attend.

.... Secretary

The secretary, in consultation with the chairman, prepares the agenda for circulation with the notice. The good chairman plans the agenda carefully. First he invites discussion items for inclusion in the agenda from those who are going to attend.

The agenda is the programme of events. The order of items is significant, because despite the best intentions, discussion of every item is not always possible. The most important issues should appear early on the agenda to ensure opportunity for discussion and decision making.

Ideally, all the items are discussed but sometimes meetings drag on or go off at a tangent. They do this because the chairman has not had the strength or skill to prevent it happening. Often dominant, articulate members attempt to take over. They do not do this for sinister purposes. It just happens that their communication skills are better than those of others present.

An agenda usually includes:

- Title of the Committee
- Place, time and date of the meeting
- Purpose of the meeting
- Minutes of the last meeting
- Matters arising from the last meeting
- Items for discussion
- Any other business
- Place, time and date of next meeting

At the meetings of some clubs or societies, the chairman invites a member to read a prayer or invocation immediately after proclaiming that the meeting is in session.

Examples: 'We the members and guests of the Knightsbridge Speakers' Club give thanks for an evening of good speaking, good listening and above all good fellowship.'

The invocation is not usually entered as an item on the Agenda. Another item that takes place but does not appear on the Agenda is the Chairman's welcome to new members appointed to the committee.

But the following items do appear on a Chairman's Agenda. The Chairman's Agenda (see Fig. 8.2) is a detailed route map through the meeting. It is a checklist of meeting matters, in sequence. By ticking off each item as it is dealt with, the chairman has a ready indicator of items still to be covered.

Support documentation is frequently required at meetings. Usually it is necessary that copies of documents such as reports, letters and financial statements be circulated in advance of the

- Declare meeting open
- Describe purpose of meeting
- Thank host for facilities (if away from home venue)
- Welcome new members
- Apologies for absence
- Secretary's report of last meeting
- Matters arising
- Business item No. 1. Invite member's report
- Invite discussion
- Summarise
- Vote
- Thank member for report
- Business item No. 2
- Business item No. 3
- Business item No. 4
- Summarise achievement by committee. Relate to objectives
- Any other business
- Agree time, place and date of next meeting
- Thank all for attending. Close meeting.

FIG. 8.2 *Format of Chairman's Agenda*

meeting. Making things run smoothly is often not easy. Information, documentary contributions and confirmation of attendance have to be grudgingly extracted from committee members with busy timetables.

In preparation for equipping and using the meeting room a checklist is helpful:

- copy of agenda for all
- table and chairs
- copies of all item-reference documentation
- paper/pens/ashtrays
- refreshments

[108]

- flip chart
- audio-visual equipment
- notification of meeting to telephone switchboard
- transport/car parking arrangements.

During the meeting itself the major documentation interest is towards the preparation of minutes. The secretary records everything that takes place:

- the names of members attending
- topics discussed
- concise details of arguments for and against
- motions carried and rejected
- names of all proposers and seconders
- voting details
- responsibility for actions recommended by the committee

If the chairman is good, he or she summarises frequently. This makes the secretary's task easier. If there is no secretary the chairman must take notes from which to produce the subsequent minutes. Ideally minutes are typed up and distributed within 48 hours of a meeting. It is helpful to include a narrow column on the right hand side of the page. The initials of members indicates at a glance responsibility for actions to be carried out or comments recorded.

CONTROL

Question: What pitfalls does a committee chairman encounter?

At many meetings there are pitfalls that the chairman has to overcome. They are everyday situations, in themselves innocuous, that can impede progress.

If there is no secretary the chairman must take notes

Pitfall – Lateness. Not all designated members are present. If the meeting is formal or important, or the first that the chairman is to convene, it is important to establish the authority of the chairman from the outset.

Action. The chairman bangs with the gavel for attention. 'Ladies and Gentlemen. This meeting has been scheduled to commence at 3.00 p.m. As there are still three persons to arrive, we will delay starting for ten minutes.' Inaction on the part of the chairman reflects lack of control.

When the meeting has to commence without the full complement of members, latecomers usually slide into their places with a mumbled apology to the chairman. The chairman interrupts proceedings at an appropriate moment to summarise the events that have taken place.

Pitfall – Random seating arrangements can diminish the contri-

bution of isolated or timid members. Relationships established through friendship or work contact give rise to strong bonds. A relaxed, well-integrated clique may separate the chairman from a new member, or the single representative of a department. If this person is nervous, and easily daunted, he or she simply remains silent.

Action. The seating arrangement is planned in advance. Dominant members are separated and placed around the table or the room. In this way the conversational focus moves from side to side.

Pitfall – Inadequate time to complete discussion of all items on the agenda. Despite the best of intentions progress is slow. Example: 'Actions arising from the minutes of the last meeting' is the subject of heated and protracted discussion. A projected time span of, say, three minutes is being considerably extended.

Action. When it is clear to the chairman that discussion is likely to prevent the present issue being resolved quickly, the authority of the chair is introduced. 'Ladies and Gentlemen. Discussion on this present issue is preventing us from moving on to the scheduled agenda items. In the context of the time available we must restrict the present discussion to a limit of five further minutes.'

Pitfall – Meeting is dominated by the personality or status of the chairman.

Action. Powerful men or women are not unaware of their own strength. But the effect they have on others is sometimes overlooked or forgotten. If the answer to the question 'Am I strong and determined and not always tolerant?' is an honest 'Yes', it is time to appraise self performance. The strength that sweeps everything aside does not always allow decision making to reflect the opinions of all parties.

Pitfall – Group of committee members who are particularly friendly sit together and create a formidable clique. Lone committee members sitting at a distance from the chairman with the clique between are dominated and subdued.

Action. Before the meeting the chairman decides on a seating plan. The most articulate members and those with a particularly aggressive lobby are distributed around the meeting table.

Pitfall – Chairman is not really sure how long the meeting is going to last.

Action. Each major item on the chairman's agenda is given a projected time. This is pencilled in. In this way progress is monitored at all stages of the meeting.

Pitfall – The chairman has a strong interest in the outcome of a particular discussion. It is likely that such interest is known by some or all of the committee members. It may influence comment for political reasons.

Action. The chairman must be impartial. In addition, he or she must be seen to be impartial. 'Ladies and Gentlemen. I imagine you all know this issue is one very close to my heart. It is therefore inappropriate for me to comment. My task as chairman is to be impartial, and that is the stance I am adopting'.

AN EFFECTIVE FORMAT

Question: What format ensures a good meeting?

Successful meetings do not just happen. Pre-planning and controlled action throughout are necessary. There are six steps:

The Six Stages of a Meeting

Stage 1. Planning

Set objectives. Decide what can be achieved in the context of the time available before the meeting, and the time that can be allocated for the meeting itself.

Identify and carry out pre-meeting tasks. Obtain relevant published reports or literature. Book venue, audio-visual equipment, car park spaces and refreshments. Book visiting speaker if appropriate.

Identify all persons who should attend.

Stage 2. Preparing

Make a note of all the topics to be covered. Prepare an initial checklist to ensure that nothing is left out.

Decide on the order of priorities. Those topics for which discussion and a decision are essential should be dealt with at an early stage. Political and behavioural considerations may intrude too. It may be inappropriate to discuss certain items too early if there is a likelihood of important contributors being late or being influenced by the tempo of earlier meetings.

Compile evidence. Products, reports, balance sheets or any other items pertinent to the meeting discussion have to be available.

Collect support documentation. Questionnaire forms, or any documentation that members must complete during or after the meeting.

Set out a clear agenda. The agenda is a programme of the main events of the meeting.

Write out the chairman's agenda. This is a detailed schedule of every meeting activity in ordered sequence for the chairman to follow.

Stage 3. Notifying all who should attend

The purpose of the meeting.

Agenda.

Time, place and date.

Stage 4. Controlling

Allocation of time. The chairman apportions the time that ideally is to be allocated to each agenda item.

Managing dominant and timid members. The input of articulate, confident members has to be balanced to include that of members with less forceful personalities.

One speaker at a time. Cross-talk and discussion within small cliques is counter-productive to the progress of a meeting.

Deflecting irrelevance. Argument and comment moving away from the topic or motion under discussion must be contained and redirected.

Stage 5. Concluding

Summarising.

Voting.

Stage 6. Recording

Preparation of the minutes. The minutes record all persons present, what has been discussed, conclusions reached and those party to the different discussions. They also record responsibility for action to be undertaken following the meeting, and the time, date and place of the next meeting.

Distribution of minutes. Ideally minutes are distributed within 48 hours to all who attended the meeting.

FORMALITIES IN MEETINGS

Question: What are the principal formal aspects of a meeting?

There are a few technicalities of meetings that are sometimes used loosely without deference to full procedural implications. So in this section the formal aspects of conducting meetings are considered.

Standing Orders

There is a code of practice that describes how meetings for limited companies and for public authorities be conducted. They are known as Standing Orders. Standing Orders are permanent regulations and cannot be varied or disregarded without formal notice.

But there is an escape route for emergency situations. The mechanism is a vote that Standing Orders be suspended. For example, Standing Orders may require that a meeting is held on a certain day – the third Monday of the month.

'Mr. French moves that Standing Orders be suspended, in order that the date of the next meeting be Tuesday 22nd. Will those in favour please raise their hands.'

Point of Order

When meetings abide by rules, it is the Chair that keeps order. Sometimes, members wish to challenge the way that the chairman keeps order. All disputes are made by members through a point of order.

'On a point of order, Mr. Chairman, why. . . .?' The chair then rules as to whether the point stands.

Sometimes points of order are used as delaying tactics. The chairman must be firm in the manner of meeting such points.

Motion

A motion is a proposal moved by a member. Formally it must be in writing, signed by the mover and handed to the chairman of a meeting. Standing Orders for most meetings require that a motion be proposed and seconded before a vote be taken. So after a motion is proposed the chairman calls for a seconder, if such a person is not known to him. A good chairman allocates a time in minutes to the proposer and seconder to state their cases. Similarly, those wishing to speak against the motion are asked to respect a time curtailment.

A motion is not usually proposed if it does not appear on the agenda. For any issue important enough to carry a vote there must be adequate time for preparation or reflection. When a committee votes on a motion and resolves to accept it, the motion becomes a resolution. In the minutes the appropriate wording is always 'It is resolved that . . .'

Amendment
Generally, amendments seek to do one of the following:
(a) to omit certain words
(b) to omit certain words and insert others
(c) to insert certain words

Voting takes place as to whether a proposed amendment should be carried. The effect is to alter the original motion. When the amendment is carried the motion is again put to the meeting as altered, but without being again proposed and seconded.

When the rules so provide, amendments are proposed and seconded. More than one amendment can be proposed to any motion.

Closure
There are various procedural motions designed to halt or impede discussion and decision making. Formally, a proposal is worded. 'Mr. Chairman. I propose that the Question now be put.' This is seconded and a vote taken. If carried, the motion under discussion is put to the vote at once, without opportunity for further debate.

Less formally, a member simply proposes 'Mr. Chairman. I propose that we now put this matter to the vote'.

Voting
The usual methods of casting votes are:

(1) Verbally. The chairman says 'All in favour say "Aye"'. He listens to the volume of assent. 'Those of you against say "No"'. The

chairman interpreting the decision on the basis of the volume of sound announces that the Ayes or the Noes have it. Usually verbal vote casting is the method adopted when the chairman senses that the decision is unanimous.

(2) By show of hands. Each person has one vote. If there are large abstentions they are noted. When the numbers voting are large, counting is necessary only when there is an equal balance on each side.

(3) By division. A count is taken of members going into different rooms set aside for the purpose.

(4) By poll. Each member has the opportunity of casting his or her vote. The poll may be conducted by meeting or by post.

SUMMARY

Question: Why are different meetings different?

Answer: Meetings differ as a function of the objectives that are being met. The different kinds of meetings are: Advisory, bargaining, collegiate, command, committee and company meetings.

Question: What documentation is necessary for conducting meetings?

Answer: The principal documentation for a meeting is (1) notice of the meeting, (2) Agenda, (3) Chairman's agenda, (4) minutes recording the names of all present, matters discussed and by whom, decisions reached, voting, tasks allocated, arrangements for next meeting and (5) administrative checklist for preparation of meeting room.

Question: What pitfalls does a committee chairman encounter?

Answer: The pitfalls encountered by a chairman at a meeting are insidious. Individually encountered they pose little threat. But cumulatively, or if they go unchecked, they disrupt meetings. Pitfalls are lateness, timidity and apprehension of new members, members who will not stop talking, lack of time control and lack of meeting discipline. Other pitfalls are sometimes the personality strength and the personal objectives of the chairman of the committee.

Question: What format ensures a good meeting?

Answer: There are six stages to a meeting. They are planning, preparing, notifying all who should attend, controlling, concluding and recording.

Question: What are the principal formal aspects of a meeting?

Answer: In the formal conduct of meetings there are Standing Orders. These set out the procedures to be observed. The chairman of the meeting is questioned on aspects of the conduct of the meeting through the raising of a 'point of order'. Motions are proposals put forward and seconded on which members then vote. Amendments, when proposed seconded and adopted, introduce changes to the wording and structure of any motion proposed. Voting is the procedure through which the members of a meeting indicate their opinion.

9

REPORT WRITING

QUESTIONS

What is the factor common to different kinds of reports?

What tasks must be carried out in the planning stage of a report?

What structure forms the basis of the majority of reports?

What cosmetic techniques make report reading easy?

What extra application is demanded by a major report?

What is the way to ensure that a report meets all critical criteria?

A COMMON FACTOR

Question: What is the factor common to different kinds of reports?

All reports describe. Some provide in-depth research data. Most draw conclusions. Many provide recommendations. Most provide a summary. Report writing covers a wide span, ranging from the simple memorandum through progress reports, routine reports, annual reports, research reports, technological reports, marketing/production/financial/administrative reports to the specialist report.

There is no special order of importance or merit. Reports differ because they are written for different purposes: because they are written for different decision makers. The common factor of different reports is that they must be tailored for their target audience. An example is given of a memorandum and a specialist report – the first and the last in the list above. Each relates to the same circumstances.

Scenario – typical domestic scene.

Wife: 'George!'

Husband: 'Yes, Daisy?'

Wife: 'What shall I wear to the party over my dress?'

Example 1

MEMORANDUM

To: Daisy

From: George

Date: Saturday

Distribution: Daisy, daughters

Subject: Fred's Party, 6, High Street.

Please take raincoat.

The memorandum gives instructions for an action that is to take place. Headings identify specifically all pertinent factors:

- the person to whom the memorandum is addressed
- all who are to be aware of the contents
- the name of the sender
- the date
- the subject matter

Memoranda are an excellent method of reporting or instructing when the formal structure of a letter is superfluous.

Example 2 Specialist report

George has received his instructions. He carefully considers his exact terms of reference, then decides on his sources of information. He collects his information, rejects what is irrelevant, analyses the rest and reaches his conclusion. He is then ready to set it out neatly because, of course, Daisy will still be doing her hair.

First he does the front page:

Report Title:	Outerwear Garment Selection
Period Covered by Report:	Saturday evening
Date:	Saturday
Author:	George
Distribution:	Daisy, daughters

Then the inside page:

Summary:	George investigated all facts, deliberated and made recommendation for selection of raincoat.
Introduction:	George and Daisy are invited to local party on Saturday evening. Daisy is

	unable to make decision in respect of outerwear selection. She invites George to consider the matter and tell her what to wear.
Terms of Reference:	Selection of outerware garment from existing clothing range within household.
Research:	Looking out of window. Tapping barometer. Reading newspaper weather report.
Research yield:	Approaching cumulus clouds identified. Prevailing wind S.E. moderate. Barometer dropping rapidly. Forecast is 'wet'.
Conclusion:	Rain is imminent.
Recommendation:	Daisy is to select and wear raincoat.

PLANNING

Question: What tasks must be carried out in the planning stage of a report?

There are three distinct stages to a report – planning, structure and cosmetic techniques. Each is important. Each one contributes directly to the success of the report.

Planning
In this stage the groundwork is laid. The most important decision is who the report is for. The language of the report, the objectives and the recommendations are addressed to the intended party. For example, middle management are likely to be concerned with pre-cise detail, as against senior management who are more interested in strategic and financial implications.

In the planning stage there are the following tasks:

(1) Define the audience to whom the report is addressed. It is appropriate to decide on the degree of confidentiality, and the level of security that should be given to the report. The extent of knowledge already possessed by the audience must be assessed too.

(2) Set objectives. The objectives are of prime importance. The parameters of the objectives become the Terms of Reference. When the report is not speculative, but is prepared for a sponsor, the objectives may be subject to negotiation between sponsor and author.

(3) Define all the information needed.

(4) Research to identify whether the report has already been published elsewhere.
   There is an International Directory of Published Market Research sponsored by the Department of Trade and Industry. It relates to published market research for products and services in world markets. Trade associations and the governing Institutes and Associations of the professions can advise in respect of related published reports.

(5) Plan for data collection.

STRUCTURE

Question: What structure forms the basis of the majority of reports?

The arrangement of material in a report depends on the purpose of the report and the expected readership. Sometimes there are existing conventions and standards: sometimes a house style. The following structure is a useful working format for any report. When appropriate, sections may be omitted or added, guided by the logic of the material to be presented. On occasion it is appropriate to change the wording of the section headings.

Report Model

Title page   This should show

        a. Title

        b. Author's name

        c. Sponsoring organisation

        d. Report number, if appropriate

        e. Date of publication

        f. Distribution

        g. Period covered by report, if appropriate

Summary   The summary is a concise, informative description of the entire work covering the objectives, investigation, conclusions and recommendations.

Table of contents   The principal headings are listed in the same words and in the same order as they appear in the report, together with the page number on which each of them begins. Lists of illustrations, tables and appendices are included.

Terms of reference   The nature and extent of the objectives are clearly defined.

Introduction	This section contains the background information needed by the reader. Included are:

    a. the purpose of the report

    b. historical background

    c. other background information needed by the least informed reader

    d. limitations of treatment and approach

    e. assumptions made

Method of investigation   The method of data collection is described. Experiments and analytical methods adopted are given.

Facts   Material, data and experimental findings are given without interpretation or inference. The opinions of others are permissible provided that the source is acknowledged. Where the quantity of material is large, a summary is given within the text, and the mass of detail is provided in an appendix.

Discussion   The discussion is a commentary on results obtained, with interpretation and reasoned argument. In many reports the discussion is not given as a separate heading, but forms part of the conclusion.

Conclusions   Conclusions are clear and orderly. They are the deductions reached after full consideration of the results obtained.

Recommendations   Recommendations are positive lines of action that in the opinion of the author follow on from the conclusions reached.

Acknowledgements   Help given in the preparation of the report and any relevant permission granted is formally acknowledged.

References   In published reports a list of references is usually necessary.

Appendices   An appendix contains all material that is too big for the body of the report.

COSMETIC TECHNIQUES

Question: What cosmetic techniques make report reading easy?

Cosmetics are concerned with how the report looks. Cosmetic techniques influence the manner in which the report is presented to the reader. The prime consideration is to help the reader absorb the written content, without strain or irritation.

The long report of many pages must not be a daunting task of frightening complexity. Like the shorter report it should consist of easily digestible sections. First, the opening must be easy to understand. The report then helps the reader along in logical sequence. The following techniques contribute to a smooth presentation.

(1) Paragraphing
Paragraphs are used to break up the material into manageable lengths. The topic sentence of each paragraph usually identifies the subject matter.

THE REPORT STRUCTURE

	Title page
	Summary
	Table of contents
	Terms of reference
	Introduction
	Method of investigation
	Facts
	Discussion
	Conclusion
	Recommendations
	Acknowledgements
	References
	Appendices

(2) Layout

In presenting technical information, management reports and notes, a schematic layout is helpful. This groups the material into sections and sub-sections and, through the position on the page and the use of numbering and headings, shows the relationship of one part of the report to another. Layout is also used to emphasise particular points. An example is 'safety precautions' in operating instructions which are made to stand out boldly from the rest of the text.

Display

Margins, indentation and spaces between lines, paragraphs and sections are used to draw attention to particular parts of the text.

Numbering

There are three basic systems:

(a) A combination of Roman and Arabic numerals and letters. a1 (i) This is usually combined with progressive margin indentation as illustrated here.

(b) Decimal systems. (Example from a report on the failure of motor cars.)

2. Analysis of breakdowns on the road
2.1. Breakdowns caused by mechanical failure
$2.1.^1$ Engine failure
$2.1.^2$ Gearbox failure
$2.1.^3$ Transmission failure
$2.1.^4$ Structural failure

Not more than three digits should be used, otherwise the system becomes clumsy. And decimal sub-division should not be used for mere listing.

(c) Sequential numbering of paragraphs.
Numbering right through the whole report permits easy reference. When several reports are issued for one project, the numbering of all reports is standardised. There is one disadvan-

tage with sequential numbering. There is no provision for indicating importance or relationships. Sequential numbering is simply a supplement to page numbering.

Headings

Headings are signposts to the reader. They are important. But there has to be consistency. If material is presented under headings and sub-headings, all material must be under headings and sub-headings. Also, listed points and co-ordinated headings should have a similar grammatical structure.

Emphasis

Headings or other groups of words can be emphasised by:

(a) position on the page
(b) spacing between letters
(c) use of upper case letters
(d) underlining

(3) Dealing with statistics

Statistics are a pitfall for the unwary. They are boring. The excitement to the scientist of performance figures validating a protracted experiment does not necessarily carry to the uninformed reader. Numbers, like text, must be reduced to easily digestible sections.

There are four main options, see Fig. 9.2.

(1) Graphs

Graphs allow visual impact of trend or change. For most people the flow of the graph line is easier to absorb than a table of disparate figures.

(2) Bar Charts

Bar charts are very useful for showing comparisons. Differences or similarities are easily seen.

(3) Pie Charts

Pie charts show how component parts add up to make a whole. Percentages are easily seen. Figures can be absorbed without any stress for the non-numerate.

(4) Pictograms

Pictograms have a vivid impact. They are particularly suitable for popular general reports. In Fig. 9.2 one car represents 10,000 cars produced.

MAJOR REPORTS

Question: What extra application is demanded by a major report?

Major reports reflect skilled specialist application. Often they are the end point of weeks or months of work. The report may be all that there is to be seen in physical terms. Many pages are needed in most major reports to describe the investigation and analyse and argue from the findings. Even with ruthless pruning appendices may double or triple the body of the report. So major reports are thick and weighty.

Writing a major report is stressful. Frequently, political overtones intrude. Possibly a substantial fee is being paid and the author is determined that the sponsor perceive the report as a document of value. So attention is essential to the following aspects.

(1) Drafting

Major reports usually progress through two, three or four draft stages. The reason is that the author is reporting or interpreting the reports and interpretations of others. Each draft is distributed for comment, discussion and amendment. It is helpful to use different coloured paper for each draft stage. White is the colour of the final report.

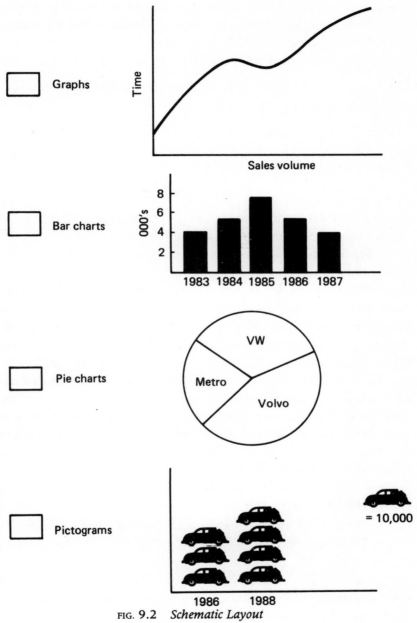

FIG. 9.2   *Schematic Layout*

(2) Detail numbering

Major reports have many sections. Each section should indicate its position in the report. Each page must indicate its position within its section. For the author this task is boring. He or she knows where each page comes, be it on computer disc or handwritten numbered page.

But extracts from reports are considered out of context. Photocopies discard the planned order and symmetry of the professionally bound report. So the author of a major report has to work hard to make each separate item of the report be identifiable in sequence from the title page to the final appendix.

(3) Appearance

All reports must be presented in a neat, professional manner. Paper quality must be good, and the report bound in hard or soft covers. There is an ample choice of binding systems on the market. But the report must look fresh and sparkling.

Imperfections in the visual aspect diminish reports considerably. Apologies for poor typewriter ribbon quality or smudged photocopies go unheard. The appearance of the report creates an attitude and an awareness even before the report is opened. With major reports the importance of the report compounds this need.

When the time comes to open the report, the title page and index set the scene. So layout and print quality warrant careful consideration. Blank white pages can be used to effect to separate and reinforce. In the body of the text the script should be on one side of a page only.

(4) Personal presentation

Whatever the strengths of the report, however great the expertise of the author, the report is inanimate. It cannot match a presentation face to face. Reports should be presented personally, not left to be read. Strict rules apply to the handing over of a report:

Rule 1. Rehearse the presentation thoroughly in advance.

Rule 2. Distribute copies of the report to all who will be present before the presentation begins.

Rule 3. Before speaking, wait for silence and full attention from all. Do not begin talking whilst people are reading. If there is silence they will look up.

Rule 4. Introduce yourself and the report title.

Rule 5. State the ground rules for the presentation

    (a) How you are going to present the material
    (b) When questions may be asked
    (c) When discussion or decision making is to take place

Rule 6. Memorise the summary of the report. Do not simply read in front of others. Continuous eye contact with all present is essential when summarising.

Reports should be handed in personally

Rule 7. Lead the listeners through the report, directing attention to the contents of appropriate pages.

AIDE MÉMOIRE

Question: What is the way to ensure that a report meets all critical criteria?

The following checklist is designed to cover all salient points relating to the design and presentation of a report.

Checklist on Report Writing

Place tick in appropriate square   YES   NO

- Have I tailored the report to the target audience?   ☐   ☐

- Have I written the report in simple, unambiguous
  language?   ☐   ☐

- Have I set out the report under the headings of
  'Introduction, Terms of Reference, Method of Investigation,
  Facts, Discussion, Conclusions and Recommendations'?   ☐   ☐

- Have I provided a summary at the beginning of the report?   ☐   ☐

- Are numbers and statistics provided in the form of graphs,
  bar charts, pie charts or pictograms?   ☐   ☐

- Has all detail material been omitted from the body of the
  report and supplied as an appendix?   ☐   ☐

	YES	NO
• Have I printed and bound the report immaculately and provided a neatly impressive title page followed by a table of contents?	☐	☐
• Have I requested a face-to-face meeting to present the report?	☐	☐

If the answer is YES, O.K. If NO, do something about it!

SUMMARY

Question: What is the factor common to different kinds of report?

Answer: The factor common to different kinds of reports is that they should all be tailored to their target audience.

Question: What tasks must be carried out in the planning stage of a report?

Answer: In the planning stage of a report the following tasks must be carried out:

(a) the target audience defined
(b) terms of reference defined
(c) the nature of all information required identified
(d) research undertaken to identify whether the report has been published elsewhere
(e) the procedures for data collection defined

Question: What structure forms the basis of the majority of reports?

Answer: An effective structure for a report incorporates:

- a title page
- a summary
- a table of contents

[135]

- terms of reference
- an introduction
- method of investigation
- facts
- discussion
- conclusions
- recommendations
- acknowledgements
- references
- appendices

Question: What cosmetic technique make report reading easy?

Answer: The cosmetic techniques that facilitate report reading are paragraphing, a layout combining display and section numbering and dealing with numbers. With numbers and statistical data there are the options of bar charts, graphs, pie charts and pictograms.

Question: What extra application is demanded by a major report?

Answer: A major report usually goes through a number of draft stages in the pathway to developing the final report. Particular attention must be directed to achieving highest standards of presentation and printing. Because of the importance of a major report, delivery should be made by a formal personal presentation.

Question: What is the way to ensure that a report meets all critical criteria?

Answer: A checklist given in the text should be used to ensure that all reports meet acceptably high standards.

PEP TALK

This is a do-it-yourself pep talk. You ask the questions. Only you can provide the answers. Communication is a two-way process. But if the messages and concepts that you send out are immaculate, they give a great lift to others in communicating well.

	YES	NO
1. Do I know what communication messages are given by my company environment?	☐	☐
2. Do I actively contribute to creating high environmental standards?	☐	☐
3. Have I helped to upgrade the opportunities for company environment administration to market the company?	☐	☐
4. Am I aware of the actual communication flow paths within the company?	☐	☐
5. Am I good at training others to communicate effectively?	☐	☐

	YES	NO
6. Do I always condense my speech scripts to short headings and trigger words written on postcard sized cards?	☐	☐
7. Do I maintain constant eye contact with my audience during a presentation?	☐	☐
8. Do I modulate my voice when delivering a speech?	☐	☐
9. Do I always smile when I pick up a telephone?	☐	☐
10. Do I answer the phone in a correct business-like manner?	☐	☐
11. Do I always prepare before making a sales call?	☐	☐
12. Do I make careful preparations before negotiating on the phone?	☐	☐
13. Do I know what public image my company should have?	☐	☐
14. Do I know the prime target audience for PR effort?	☐	☐
15. Do I know how to reach that audience?	☐	☐
16. Can I formulate an appropriate press release?	☐	☐
17. Do I know how to listen properly?	☐	☐
18. Am I assertive?	☐	☐
19. Do I know how to become more assertive?	☐	☐
20. Do I praise people for everyday tasks carried out well?	☐	☐

Pep Talk

		YES	NO
21.	Do I know how to write an agenda for a meeting?	☐	☐
22.	Can I write a Chairman's agenda?	☐	☐
23.	Can I conduct a meeting confidently?	☐	☐
24.	Am I familiar with the pitfalls likely to be encountered by the chairman of a meeting?	☐	☐
25.	Am I familiar with the formal aspects of a meeting?	☐	☐
26.	Do I know the structure that is the basis for most reports?	☐	☐
27.	Do I know what cosmetic techniques make reading reports easy?	☐	☐
28.	Do I write my reports in simple, unambiguous language?	☐	☐

RECOMMENDED READING

Back, K. & K., *Assertiveness at Work*, McGraw Hill, 1982

Bland, M., *Be Your Own PR Man*, Kogan Page, 2nd edn. 1987

Curry, T. P. E., Sykes, J. R. and Heslop, P. L., *The Conduct of Meetings*, Jordans, 1982

Katz, B., *How to Win More Business By Phone, Telex and Fax*, Century Hutchinson, 1987

Katz, B., *How to Manage Customer Service*, Gower, 1987

Katz, B., *How to Market Professional Services*, Gower, 1988

Margerison, C., *Conversation Control Skills for Managers*, Mercury, 1987

Maude, B., *Practical Communication for Managers*, Longman, 1974

INDEX